ATMA BODHA FOR BEGINNERS

WORD-TO-WORD MEANING, AND COMMENTARY ON ĀDI ŚANKARĀCĀRYA'S TREATISE

RAJEEV KURAPATI

ISBN
Paperback 979-8-89929-869-1
Hardcase 979-8-89961-338-8

Author's Note

In offering this translation of *Ātma Bodha,* my aim is to make the timeless teachings of *Ādi Śaṅkarācārya* accessible to readers of today. In preparing this translation, I have referenced the works of esteemed philosophers such as Swami Chinmayananda and Swami Nikhilananda. I have also consulted traditional Sanskrit sources (listed at the end of this book) to ensure that the translation remains true to the original teachings of *Ādi Śaṅkarācārya,* providing an accurate and accessible interpretation of this profound treatise.

This translation is a reflection of the collective wisdom, support, and inspiration I have received, and I am deeply grateful to all who have been a part of this journey.

A heartfelt thanks to Sheelu Kashyap, whose creative vision has added a unique touch to this book's design, making it not just a text, but an experience.

With deep gratitude,
Rajeev Kurapati

असतो मा सद्गमय ।
तमसो मा ज्योतिर्गमय ।
मृत्योर्मा अमृतं गमय ॥

Lead me from untruth to truth.
Lead me from darkness to light.
Lead me from death to immortality.

A shānti mantra extracted from
Bṛhadāraṇyaka Upaniṣad (1.3.28)

Dedication

To *Ādi Śaṅkarācārya,* whose timeless wisdom continues to illuminate the path of Self-realization for countless seekers.

Contents

Disclaimer

This translation of Ātma Bodha is intended as an introductory guide and does not aim to cover all the concepts of Advaita Vedānta comprehensively. Readers seeking a more detailed understanding are encouraged to explore additional texts and resources on Advaita Vedānta. This work is designed to provide a focused exploration of Ādi Śaṅkarācārya's treatise, emphasizing accessibility and clarity for readers.

~

About the Book

Ātma Bodha, meaning "Self Knowledge," is one of the foundational texts of Advaita Vedanta by *Ādi Śaṅkarācārya.* This text provides a systematic guide to understanding the nature of the Self (Ātma) and the path to Self-realization, leading to the ultimate knowledge of one's true, eternal essence.

Ādi Śaṅkarācārya was an 8th-century Indian philosopher who consolidated Advaita Vedanta and significantly shaped Hinduism through his teachings and writings. Born in Kerala, India, Śaṅkarācārya traveled across the subcontinent, spreading his teachings, engaging in philosophical debates, and revitalizing Vedic thought. He is credited with writing numerous commentaries on ancient texts such as the Upanishads, Bhagavad Gita, and Brahma Sutras. His works, including *Ātma Bodha,* emphasize Self-realization as the path to liberation (mokṣa) and remain foundational in Indian philosophy.

Advaita Vedanta is a darśana (meaning "vision"), a school of Indian philosophy that posits a non-dualistic ontology. It teaches that the true nature of reality is a singular, unified existence. According to Advaita Vedanta, the individual Self and the ultimate reality are fundamentally of the same essence. Ultimate reality is a term used commonly to describe the concept of Brahman or Paramātma, referring to the source and foundation of all universes and everything that exists.

The multiplicity and diversity we perceive in the world, including the distinction between Self and other, are considered illusions. In this view, understanding the true nature of reality involves recognizing that all distinctions are ultimately illusory, and that everything is a projection in one unified field or essence.

One of the most distinctive features of *Ātma Bodha* is *Ādi Śaṅkarācārya*'s masterful use of analogies in nearly every verse. These analogies serve to illustrate complex philosophical concepts in a way that is accessible and relatable. For example, he uses analogies such as the Sun illuminating the world to explain how the Self illuminates the mind and senses, or how a rope mistaken for a snake illustrates the illusion of ignorance. These analogies not only clarify the teachings but also engage the reader, making the text more memorable and impactful.

Through metaphors and logical reasoning, *Ādi Śaṅkarācārya* elucidates how ignorance (*avidyā*) veils the true Self and how knowledge (*jñāna*) dissolves this ignorance, leading to liberation (*mokṣa*). The text emphasizes practices like discernment, meditation, and detachment to cultivate Self-awareness and realize one's unity with Brahman, the ultimate reality.

Ātma Bodha has 68 verses. Here is a brief summary of the text divided based on the verses:

Path of Knowledge (Verses 1-8)

❧ **Verses 1-2:** The text begins by emphasizing the importance of Self-knowledge (*Ātma-Bodha*) for liberation (mokṣa). Just as fire is necessary to burn fuel, Self-knowledge is essential to destroy ignorance (avidyā).

❧ **Verses 3-8:** These verses describe the qualifications needed for pursuing the path of knowledge, such as discrimination (viveka), dispassion (vairāgya), and a burning desire for liberation (mumukṣutva). The true nature of the Self is introduced as distinct from the body and mind.

Nature of the Self (Verses 9-16)

❧ **Verses 9-12:** The Self is described as eternal, pure consciousness, and the substratum of all that exists. It is beyond the physical body, senses, mind, and intellect, and is the witness of all experiences.

🌸 **Verses 13-16:** The text explains that the Self is not subject to change, birth, or death, and is untainted by worldly experiences. It is the source of all light and knowledge, much like the Sun illuminates the world.

Nature of the World (Verses 17-29)

🌸 **Verses 17-22:** The concept of māyā (illusion) is introduced. The world and the individual Self (Jīva) are seen as projections of māyā, which conceals the true nature of the Self.

🌸 **Verses 23-29:** These verses discuss the superimposition (adhyāsa) of the non-Self (anātma) on the Self, leading to the illusion of individuality. The text uses analogies like the rope mistaken for a snake to illustrate how ignorance causes misperception.

Path to Realization (Verses 30-40)

🌸 **Verses 30-34:** The text describes the process of negating the non-Self (*neti-neti*, "not this, not this") to realize the true Self. Through discrimination, the seeker differentiates between the real (the Self) and the unreal (the world).

❦ **Verses 35-40:** The importance of meditation (dhyāna) on the Self is emphasized. By focusing the mind on the true nature of the Self, the seeker overcomes ignorance and realizes their true identity as Brahman, the ultimate reality.

State of Realization (Verses 41-57)

❦ **Verses 41-46:** These verses describe the state of realization where the seeker sees everything as a manifestation of the Self. The distinctions between knower, knowledge, and known dissolve.

❦ **Verses 47-50:** The realized soul (jñānī) experiences supreme bliss (ānanda) and remains unaffected by the dualities of the world, such as pleasure and pain, success and failure.

❦ **Verses 51-57:** The liberated person (Jīvanmukta) lives in the world without attachment, knowing that the Self alone is real and everything else is an illusion. The text contrasts the state of bondage with the state of liberation.

Conclusion and Final Teachings (Verses 58-68)

🌱 **Verses 58-63:** The final verses emphasize the universality and all-pervading nature of the Self. The text reiterates that Self-realization leads to the dissolution of all bondage and the experience of immortality (amṛta).

🌱 **Verses 64-68:** The text concludes by encouraging the seeker to focus on the Self, the ultimate reality, which is beyond time, space, and causality. The state of realization is described as one of eternal, unchanging bliss.

Ātma Bodha guides the seeker from ignorance to knowledge, from illusion to reality, and ultimately to liberation. By realizing the true nature of the Self as Brahman, one transcends all limitations and attains eternal peace and bliss.

Anubandha Chatuṣṭayam for Ātma Bodha

The Anubandha Chatuṣṭayam refers to the four prerequisites traditionally addressed in Indian philosophical texts to define the purpose and scope of the work. For *Ātma Bodha,* these can be out lined as follows:

1. **Adhikārī (Eligible Seeker):** Like other texts of Advaita Vedānta, this text is intended for seekers on the path of nivṛtti (inward-oriented renunciation and contemplation), dedicated to the pursuit of self-realization. It is not meant for those engaged in pravṛtti (outward-oriented actions and pursuits). The seeker must possess a genuine interest in attaining self-realization.

2. **Viṣaya (Subject Matter):** The subject matter of *Ātma Bodha* is the nature of the self (Ātman) and its distinction from the non-self. It teaches the ultimate reality of Brahman and the illusory nature of the world.

3. **Prayojana (Purpose):** The purpose of the text is to lead the seeker to mokṣa (liberation) by imparting self-knowledge (ātma-jñāna) and dispelling ignorance (ajñāna), which is the root cause of bondage.

4. **Sambandha (Relationship):** The relationship between the text and its subject matter is instructional. The text serves as a means to impart the knowledge of the self, which is the ultimate goal. It acts as a bridge between the seeker's ignorance and realization.

Ātma Bodha belongs to a category of Sanskrit texts known as prakarana granthas, which provide a systematic and simplified exposition of the core principles of a philosophical truth. These texts often serve as introductory or explanatory works. In the context of Advaita Vedānta, prakarana granthas are designed to make complex concepts accessible to seekers by focusing on specific aspects of the philosophy, such as self-knowledge (ātma-jñāna) or the nature of reality. They prepare seekers for deeper study of foundational texts like the Upaniṣads, Bhagavad Gītā, and Brahma Sūtras. Notable examples of such texts include *Ātma Bodha*, Tattva Bodha, and Vivekachūḍāmaṇi.

Key Concepts in Advaita Vedanta

There are few important concepts in Advaita Vedanta that would benefit from a brief explanation before diving into the word-to-word meanings and translations of *Ātma Bodha*. Understanding these concepts will provide a foundation for comprehending the deeper teachings of the text.

Ātma

The Ātma is roughly translated as the inner Self, which is distinct from the body, mind, and ego. In Advaita Vedanta, the Ātma is considered identical with Brahman, the ultimate reality. Realizing the Ātma is the goal of human life according to Advaita. The text teaches that Ātma is eternal, pure consciousness, and the substratum of all existence.

Brahman

Brahman is the unchanging, infinite, immanent, and transcendent reality that is the essence of the universe.

It is beyond attributes (nirguṇa) and forms the basis of all that exists. Brahman is the ultimate reality with which the Ātma is identified. Realizing the non-difference between Ātma and Brahman is the essence of Self-realization.

Māyā

Māyā is the illusion that veils the true nature of reality and causes the perception of the duality in the world. It is the inherent power or attribute of Brahman, known as Brahman's shakti (power). It is through māyā that the one, non-dual Brahman appears as the diverse universe. Understanding māyā is crucial because it explains why people perceive themselves as separate individuals (Jīvas) rather than recognizing their true identity as Brahman.

Avidyā and Jñāna

Avidyā refers to the ignorance of one's true nature as the Ātma. It is this ignorance that leads to the identification with the body, mind, and ego, and thus, to the experience of samsāra (the cycle of birth and death).

The removal of avidyā through knowledge (jñāna) is the primary focus of *Ātma Bodha*. It is ignorance that binds the individual soul, and knowledge that liberates it.

Jñāna refers to the direct knowledge or realization of the Self as non-different from Brahman. It is not mere intellectual understanding but a profound inner experience of truth. Jñāna is the means to mokṣa (liberation). It dispels avidyā and leads to the realization that "I am Brahman" (Aham Brahmāsmi).

Jīva

Jīva is another name for the individual Self. Due to ignorance, the Jīva identifies with the body and mind and experiences the world as a separate entity. The Jīva, under the influence of māyā and avidyā, forgets its true nature as Ātma. Realization involves the understanding that the Jīva is not separate from Brahman.

Understanding these concepts is crucial to grasp the teachings presented in the verses of *Ātma Bodha*.

Word to Word Meaning, Translation and Commentary

तपोभिः क्षीणपापानां शान्तानां वीतरागिणाम् ।
मुमुक्षूणामपेक्ष्योऽयमात्मबोधो विधीयते ॥

tapobhiḥ kṣīṇapāpānāṃ śāntānāṃ vītarāgiṇām ।
mumukṣūṇāmapekṣyo'yamātmabodho vidhīyate ॥

तपोभिः (tapobhiḥ): through austerities and spiritual practices; क्षीणपापानाम् (kṣīṇapāpānām): of those whose karmic impediments have been diminished or who have attenuated their negative tendencies; शान्तानाम् (śāntānām): of those who have attained inner tranquility; वीतरागिणाम् (vītarāgiṇām): of those who are free from worldly attachments and transcended passions; मुमुक्षूणाम् (mumukṣūṇām): of those intensely desiring liberation; अपेक्ष्यः (apekṣyaḥ): is to be sought after or desired; अयम् (ayam): this; आत्मबोधः (Ātmabodhaḥ): Self-knowledge; विधीयते (vidhīyate): is prescribed.

> **This knowledge of the Self is meant for those who have purified themselves through austerities, who are peaceful, free from worldly attachments, and who earnestly seek liberation.**

The first verse introduces the context in which Self-knowledge (*Ātma Bodha*) becomes possible. The verse states that Self-knowledge is prescribed for those who have purified their sins through austerities (tapas), are peaceful, free from attachment (vītarāga), and possess a strong desire for liberation (mumukṣu).

In this verse, tapas refers to disciplined spiritual practices that help purify the mind and body, leading to the diminishing of past sins (pāpa). A peaceful mind is one that has subdued the fluctuations caused by desires, emotions, and distractions. Vītarāga describes those who have transcended worldly attachments and cravings, allowing for deeper inner focus. Importantly, the verse highlights mumukṣu, the sincere longing for liberation (mokṣa), as a key qualification for receiving and understanding *Ātma Bodha*.

The verse suggests that only when one achieves these states of mental purity, detachment, and inner peace through spiritual practices, does the journey toward Self-realization and understanding the true nature of the Self become fruitful.

~

बोधोऽन्यसाधनेभ्यो हि साक्षान्मोक्षैकसाधनम् ।
पाकस्य वह्निवज्ज्ञानं विना मोक्षो न सिध्यति ॥

bodho'nyasādhanebhyo hi sākṣān-mokṣaika-sādhanam ।
pākasya vahnivaj-jñānaṃ vinā mokṣo na sidhyati ॥

बोधः (bodhaḥ): knowledge or realization; अन्यसाधनेभ्यः (anyasādhanebhyaḥ): than other means or methods; हि (hi): indeed; साक्षात् (sākṣāt): directly; मोक्षैकसाधनम् (mokṣaika-sādhanam): the sole means to liberation; पाकस्य (pākasya): for cooking; वह्निः (vahniḥ): fire; वत् (vat): like; ज्ञानम् (jñānam): knowledge; विना (vinā): without; मोक्षः (mokṣaḥ): liberation; न (na): not; सिध्यति (sidhyati): achieved.

> **Self-knowledge is the most direct path to liberation, surpassing all other methods. Just as fire is necessary for cooking, knowledge is essential for attaining liberation.**

This verse underscores the supreme role of knowledge (jñāna) in achieving liberation (mokṣa). While various spiritual practices exist, knowledge is presented as the most direct and essential path to liberation.

The analogy of fire for cooking powerfully illustrates this idea. Just as fire is necessary to transform raw food into a cooked meal, knowledge is vital for transforming ignorance into enlightenment. Without fire, cooking is impossible; likewise, without knowledge, liberation cannot be attained. This highlights that while other practices may support the journey, knowledge remains the indispensable key to true freedom.

अविरोधितया कर्म नाविद्यां विनिवर्तयेत् ।
विद्याऽविद्यां निहन्त्येव तेजस्तिमिरसङ्घवत् ॥

avirōdhitayā karma nāvidyāṃ vinivartayet ।
vidyā'vidyāṃ nihantyēva tējastimira-saṅghavat ॥

अविरोधितया (avirōdhitayā): (since it is) not in opposition; कर्म (karma): action; न (na): not; अविद्याम् (avidyāṃ): ignorance; विनिवर्तयेत् (vinivartayet): can remove; विद्या (vidyā): knowledge; अविद्याम् (avidyāṃ): ignorance; निहन्ति (nihanti): destroys; एव (eva): indeed; तेजः (tejaḥ): light; तिमिर (timira): darkness; सङ्घवत् (saṅghavat): like a multitude.

> **Karma (action), which is not opposed to ignorance, cannot remove it. Only knowledge can destroy ignorance, just as light dispels darkness.**

This verse highlights the distinct roles of action (karma) and knowledge (vidyā) in attaining spiritual liberation. It explains that actions, though useful for preparing the mind and fostering discipline, cannot remove ignorance because they are not inherently opposed to it. Rituals, ethical deeds, and daily duties, while beneficial, do not address the root cause of ignorance.

In contrast, knowledge is directly opposed to ignorance (avidyā), just as light is to darkness. Knowledge alone has the intrinsic power to dispel ignorance, as darkness disappears when light is present. This demonstrates that while actions can aid in mental preparation, only knowledge can directly eliminate ignorance and lead to liberation.

परिच्छिन्न इवाज्ञानात्तन्नाशे सति केवलः ।
स्वयं प्रकाशते ह्यात्मा मेघापायेंऽशुमानिव ॥

paricchinna ivājñānāt tannāśe sati kevalaḥ ।
svayaṃ prakāśate hyātmā meghāpāye'ṃśumān iva ॥

परिच्छिन्न (paricchinna): limited; इव (iva): as if; अज्ञानात् (ajñānāt): due to ignorance; तन्नाशे (tannāśe): upon its destruction; सति (sati): being; केवलः (kevalaḥ): alone, pure; स्वयम् (svayam): by itself; प्रकाशते (prakāśate): shines; हि (hi): indeed; आत्मा (Ātmā): the Self; मेघापाये (meghāpāye): when the clouds disappear; अंशुमान् (aṃśumān): the Sun; इव (iva): like.

> **The Self seems limited because of ignorance. When that ignorance is removed, the Self shines by itself, just as the Sun shines brightly when the clouds clear away.**

This verse explains how ignorance (ajñāna) obscures the true Self (Ātma), making it appear limited and bound by physical and mental constraints. Ignorance creates a false sense of individuality, causing the infinite Self to seem finite. Once ignorance is destroyed, the Self's true nature is revealed as pure and unconditioned ("kevala"), unaffected by previous limitations.

The verse highlights that the Self is Self-luminous, requiring no external source of illumination. It uses the metaphor of the Sun and clouds: just as the Sun is always shining but appears hidden when clouds cover it, the Self is always present and radiant, yet seems concealed by ignorance. When ignorance is removed, the Self shines forth in its full brilliance.

अज्ञानकलुषं जीवं ज्ञानाभ्यासाद्विनिर्मलम् ।
कृत्वा ज्ञानं स्वयं नश्येज्जलं कतकरेणुवत् ॥

ajñānakaluṣaṃ jīvaṃ jñānābhyāsādvinirmalam ।
kṛtvā jñānaṃ svayaṃ naśyejjalaṃ katakareṇuvat ॥

अज्ञान (ajñāna): ignorance; कलुषम् (kaluṣam): impure; जीवम् (jīvam): individual jīva-ātmā; ज्ञानाभ्यासात् (jñānābhyāsāt): through the practice of knowledge; विनिर्मलम् (vinirmalam): pure; कृत्वा (kṛtvā): having made; ज्ञानम् (jñānam): knowledge; स्वयम् (svayaṃ): itself; नश्येत् (naśyet): disappears जलम् (jalam): water; कतकरेणुवत् (katakareṇuvat): like the clearing nut powder.

> **The Self, tainted by ignorance, becomes pure through repeated practice of knowledge. Then, this knowledge itself vanishes, just as the clearing nut dissolves after purifying water.**

This verse highlights the transformative power of knowledge (jñāna) in the spiritual journey. It describes the individual soul (jīva-ātma) as impure due to ignorance (ajñāna), caused by identifying with the body, mind, and ego. This ignorance obscures the true nature of the Ātmā. Through the diligent practice of knowledge (jñānābhyāsa), the jīva-ātma is purified (vinirmalam), shedding false identifications and revealing one's true nature.

The verse uses the metaphor of the clearing nut (kataka) to illustrate the role of knowledge. Just as the nut purifies water by removing impurities and then settles down, knowledge purifies the jīva-ātma and becomes unnecessary once ignorance is dispelled. When the true Self is realized, knowledge dissolves, as ultimate realization transcends intellectual understanding and becomes a direct, experiential awareness of the Self.

"

Self-knowledge is meant for those
who have purified themselves
through spiritual practices, become
peaceful, and free from attachments.
It is especially for those with a strong
desire for liberation (moksha).

"

Self-knowledge is the most direct
path to liberation, surpassing all other
methods. Just as fire is necessary for
cooking, knowledge is essential for
attaining liberation.

संसारः स्वप्नतुल्यो हि रागद्वेषादिसङ्कुलः ।
स्वकाले सत्यवद्भाति प्रबोधे सत्यसद्भवेत् ॥

saṃsāraḥ svapnatulyo hi rāgadveṣādisaṅkulaḥ ।
svakāle satyavadbhāti prabodhe satyasadbhavet ॥

संसारः (saṃsāraḥ): the phenomenal world or the worldly existence; स्वप्नतुल्यः (svapnatulyaḥ): like a dream; हि (hi): indeed; रागद्वेषादि (rāgadveṣādi): attachment, aversion, etc.; सङ्कुलः (saṅkulaḥ): filled with; स्वकाले (svakāle): at its time; सत्यवत् (satyavat): as if real; भाति (bhāti): appears; प्रबोधे (prabodhe): upon awakening; सत्य (satya): (that which appeared as) real; असद्भवेत् (asadbhavet): becomes unreal (i.e., recognized that it was only a dream).

> **This world is like a dream, filled with attachments and aversions. It seems real while we're experiencing it, but becomes unreal when we awaken to the truth.**

This verse compares the phenomenal world (saṃsāra) to a dream (svapna), emphasizing its illusory nature. It highlights that our everyday experience, filled with attachment (rāga), aversion (dveṣa), and desires, creates a complex but ultimately unreal experience. Just as events in a dream feel real while dreaming, the verse notes that worldly phenomena seem true and compelling during their experience.

However, upon prabodha (awakening), which signifies spiritual enlightenment or the realization of the true Self, the world is recognized as unreal (asadbhavet), much like waking up from a dream and realizing its unreality. This analogy underscores the fleeting, illusory nature of worldly experiences compared to the enduring truth of spiritual awareness.

~

तावत्सत्यं जगद्भाति शुक्तिकारजतं यथा ।
यावन्न ज्ञायते ब्रह्म सर्वाधिष्ठानमद्वयम् ॥

tāvatsatyaṃ jagadbhāti śuktikārajataṃ yathā ।
yāvanna jñāyate brahma sarvādhiṣṭhānamadvayam ॥

तावत् (tāvat): until then; सत्यम् (satyaṃ): real; जगत् (jagat): world; भाति (bhāti): appears; शुक्तिका (śuktikā): mother-of-pearl (oyster shell); रजतम् (rajatam): silver; यथा (yathā): just as; यावत् (yāvat): until; न (na): not; ज्ञायते (jñāyate): is known; ब्रह्म (brahma): Brahman, the absolute; सर्व (sarva): all; अधिष्ठानम् (adhiṣṭhānam): substratum; अद्वयम् (advayam): non-dual (without a second).

> **This world seems real, like silver appearing in a pearl oyster shell, until Brahman, the one reality underlying everything, is truly known.**

This verse compares the apparent reality of the world (jagat) to the illusion of silver in mother-of-pearl, emphasizing that the world seems real (satyaṃ bhāti) only until the ultimate truth is realized. The classic Vedantic analogy of mistaking mother-of-pearl (śuktikā) for silver (rajataṃ) illustrates how we mistakenly perceive the world as real, when it is actually a projection or appearance.

Brahman is described as sarvādhiṣṭhānam (the substratum of all) and advayam (non-dual), underscoring that Brahman is the only true reality, underlying all appearances, and there is nothing separate from it. The phrase "yāvanna jñāyate" (until it is not known) indicates that the illusion of the world's independent reality is dispelled only through the direct realization of Brahman. This verse highlights the illusory nature of the world, much like the deception of silver on an oyster shell, and affirms Brahman as the sole, ultimate truth.

~

8

उपादानेऽखिलाधारे जगन्ति परमेश्वरे ।
सर्गस्थितिलयान् यान्ति बुद्बुदानीव वारिणि ॥

upādāne'khilādhāre jaganti parameśvare ।
sargasthitilayān yānti budbudānīva vāriṇi ॥

उपादाने (upādāne): in the material cause; अखिलाधारे (akhilādhāre): the support of all; जगन्ति (jaganti): the worlds; परमेश्वरे (parameśvare): in the Supreme Lord or the Brahman; सर्ग (sarga): creation; स्थिति (sthiti): sustenance; लयान् (layān): dissolution; यान्ति (yānti): undergo, experience; बुद्बुदानि (budbudāni): bubbles; इव (iva): like; वारिणि (vāriṇi): in water.

> **All worlds come into being, exist, and dissolve in the Supreme Lord, who is the source and support of everything, just like bubbles appear, exist, and vanish in water.**

This verse uses the analogy of bubbles in water to explain the relationship between the absolute reality (Brahman) and the phenomenal world. It describes Brahman or the Supreme Lord (parameśvara) as both the material cause (upādāna) and support (ādhāra) of all existence, emphasizing the non-dual nature of reality.

The worlds (jaganti) undergoes the cycles of creation, sustenance, and dissolution within this Supreme reality. Like bubbles (budbudāni) arising from and dissolving into water (vāriṇi), the worlds emerge from, exist within, and return to Brahman. This illustrates the transient, illusory nature of the phenomenal world and its intimate connection to its source.

The verse invites reflection on how the diversity we perceive is ultimately non-different from its underlying reality, encouraging seekers to look beyond worldly appearances and contemplate the true nature of reality and our place within it.

∼

9

सच्चिदात्मन्यनुस्यूते नित्ये विष्णौ प्रकल्पिताः ।
व्यक्तयो विविधाः सर्वा हाटके कटकादिवत् ॥

saccidātmayanusūte nitye viṣṇau prakalpitāḥ ।
vyaktayo vividhāḥ sarvā hāṭake kaṭakādivat ॥

सच्चिदात्मनि (saccidātmai): in the existence-consciousness-Self; अनुस्यूते (anusūte): pervading, inherent; नित्ये (nitye): eternal; विष्णौ (viṣṇau): in Vishnu (the all-pervading supreme); प्रकल्पिताः (prakalpitāḥ): imagined, manifested; व्यक्तयः (vyaktayaḥ): manifestations, forms; विविधाः (vividhāḥ): various; सर्वाः (sarvāḥ): all; हाटके (hāṭake): in gold; कटकादिवत् (kaṭakādivat): like bracelets, etc.

> **All the various forms in the universe**
> **are imagined in the eternal Vishnu**
> **(all-pervading Supreme), who is pure**
> **existence and consciousness, just like**
> **different ornaments are nothing**
> **but forms of gold.**

This verse highlights the non-dual nature of reality and the illusory nature of the phenomenal world. It identifies Vishnu as saccidātmai (existence-consciousness-self), representing Brahman, the eternal (nitye) and all-pervading ultimate reality. The various forms (vyaktayaḥ vividhāḥ) are described as prakalpitāḥ (imagined or manifested) within this eternal reality, indicating that the multitude of phenomena we perceive are superimpositions on Brahman. These forms, like waves on the ocean, are not separate from their source.

The analogy of gold (hāṭake) and ornaments (kaṭakādivat) illustrates that just as bracelets and rings are merely forms of gold, all forms in the universe are manifestations of the one non-dual reality, with no independent existence apart from it.

The verse emphasizes that the diversity of the world is an illusion (māyā) imposed on the unchanging Brahman. By recognizing this unity of existence, one attains liberation (mokṣa), realizing the Self as non-different from Brahman, the ultimate reality.

～

10

यथाकाशो हृषीकेशो नानोपाधिगतो विभुः ।
तद्भेदाद्भिन्नवद्भाति तन्नाशे केवलो भवेत् ॥

yathākāśo hṛṣīkeśo nānopādhigato vibhuḥ ।
tadbhedādbhinnavad bhāti tannāśe kevalo bhavet ॥

यथा (yathā): just as; आकाशः (ākāśaḥ): space; हृषीकेशः (hṛṣīkeśaḥ): hrishikesha (an epithet of Vishnu, literally "lord of the senses"); नाना (nānā): various; उपाधि (upādhi): limiting adjuncts; गतः (gataḥ): gone into or associated with; विभुः (vibhuḥ): all-pervading; तद्भेदात् (tadbhedāt): due to their differences; भिन्नवत् (bhinnavat): as if different; भाति (bhāti): appears; तन्नाशे (tannāśe): upon their destruction; केवलः (kevalaḥ): alone; भवेत् (bhavet): becomes.

Like space seems different when contained in various objects, the all-pervading Lord (Supreme reality) appears different due to various limiting conditions. When these conditions are removed, He remains as the One alone.

This verse uses the analogy of space (ākāśa) to explain the nature of the Supreme Reality (Brahman) and its apparent manifestation as the diverse world. Just as space is all-pervading and unaffected by the objects within it, the Supreme Self (Hrishikesha) remains undivided and unaffected by the world's diversity.

The term "upādhi" refers to limiting adjuncts that create the illusion of divisions. Just as space seems divided by containers, the Supreme Self appears diverse when associated with various forms and names. However, these differences are not inherent to the Self but arise due to the upādhis.

The phrase "tadbhedādbhinnavad bhāti" (appears as if different due to their differences) emphasizes that the perceived multiplicity is an illusion. When these limiting adjuncts are destroyed (tannāśe), the Supreme Self is realized as kevala—pure and alone. This realization dissolves all apparent diversity, revealing the non-dual nature of reality.

~

"

Jñāna is necessary for understanding one's true nature to achieve ultimate freedom. This knowledge is not merely intellectual but a profound inner realization that dispels ignorance and leads to mokṣa.

"

While actions and practices are valuable and necessary for preparing the mind, they must be complemented by the pursuit of true knowledge (jñāna) to achieve liberation (mokṣa). Knowledge is depicted as the ultimate means to eradicate ignorance, leading to the realization of the true Self and ultimate freedom. This understanding reinforces the importance of seeking wisdom and insight as the key to spiritual liberation.

11

नानोपाधिवशादेव जातिवर्णाश्रमादयः ।
आत्मन्यारोपितास्तोये रसवर्णादि भेदवत् ॥

nānopādhivaśādeva jātivarṇāśramādayaḥ ।
Ātmaārōpitāstōyē rasavarṇādi bhēdavat ॥

नानोपाधि (nānā-upādhi): various limiting adjuncts; वशात् (vaśāt): due to the influence of; एव (eva): only; जाति (jāti): caste; वर्ण (varṇa): class; आश्रम (āśrama): stage of life; आदयः (ādayaḥ): etcetera; आत्मनि (Ātmani): on the Self; आरोपिताः (āropitāḥ): superimposed; तोये (toye): in water; रस (rasa): taste; वर्ण (varṇa): color; आदि (ādi): etcetera; भेदवत् (bhēdavat): like differences.

Because of different limiting conditions, distinctions like caste, color, and life-stage are falsely attributed to the Self, just as taste, color, and other qualities are attributed to water.

This verse emphasizes the concept of superimposition (āropita) and the illusory nature of distinctions imposed on the true Self (Ātma). It explains that distinctions such as caste (jāti), class (varṇa), and stage of life (āśrama) are not inherent to the Self but are superimposed due to limiting adjuncts (upādhis).

The analogy of water illustrates this: water, which is pure and without inherent taste or color, appears different when mixed with substances. Similarly, the Self, pure consciousness, appears to have distinctions due to the influence of upādhis.

Advaita Vedanta teaches that the diversity we perceive is an illusion caused by ignorance (avidyā) and not ultimately real. The true Self is beyond all distinctions and remains unaffected by them. Seekers are encouraged to look beyond superficial differences and realize the unity of existence, understanding that distinctions are illusory. Recognizing this leads to the knowledge of the Self's undivided nature, ultimately resulting in liberation (mokṣa).

12

पंचीकृतमहाभूतसंभवं कर्मसंचितम् ।
शरीरं सुखदुःखानां भोगायतनमुच्यते ॥

pañcīkṛtamahābhūtasambhavaṃ karmasañcitam ।
śarīraṃ sukhaduḥkhānāṃ bhogāyatanamucyate ॥

पञ्चीकृत (pañcīkṛta): compounded from the five great elements; महाभूत (mahābhūta): great elements; संभवम् (sambhavam): born of, originating from; कर्म (karma): actions; सञ्चितम् (sañcitam): accumulated; शरीरम् (śarīram): the body; सुखदुःखानाम् (sukhaduḥkhānām): of pleasures and pains; भोगायतनम् (bhogāyatanam): the abode of experience; उच्यते (ucyate): is called.

> **The body, which is born of the compounded five great elements and accumulated actions, is called the abode of experience for pleasures and pains.**

This verse explains the Vedantic view of the human body and its role in life's experiences. The body is described as "pañcīkṛta-mahābhūta-sambhavam," meaning it is composed of the five great elements—earth, water, fire, air, and ether—through the process of pañcīkaraṇa. It is also called "karma-sañcitam," signifying that the body is shaped by accumulated karma (past actions), embodying the results of one's karmic history.

The body is the "bhogāyatanam," the seat of experience where one undergoes "sukhaduḥkhānām," pleasures and pains, as a consequence of past actions. It serves as the medium through which the soul experiences both joy and sorrow, acting as an instrument for reaping the fruits of karma.

Vedanta teaches that the body is a temporary vessel, not the true Self. The ultimate goal is to transcend identification with the body and realize the true nature of the Self—pure consciousness beyond physical form and dualities. This realization leads to liberation (mokṣa), where one is free from the limitations of the body and mind .

"Pañcīkaraṇam" is a concept in Vedanta philosophy that deals with the process of the creation of the physical universe from the subtle elements. It explains how the five basic elements (pañca mahābhūtas) combine to form the gross elements, which make up the physical world.

The Five Basic Elements

The five subtle elements (tanmatras) are:

1.   Ākāśa (Space)

2.   Vāyu (Air)

3.   Agni (Fire)

4.   Āpaḥ (Water)

5.   Pṛthvī (Earth)

Process of Pañcīkaraṇam

The process of pañcīkaraṇam involves the mixing and recombination of these five subtle elements to create the gross elements. Here's a step-by-step breakdown:

- **Division into Two Halves:** Each subtle element is divided into two equal parts.

- **Retention of One Half:** Each element retains one half of itself.

- **Division into Four Quarters:** The remaining half of each element is further divided into four equal parts.

- **Combination:** Each element combines with one quarter of the other four elements.

So, each gross element is formed by:

- 1/2 of its own subtle element

- 1/8 of each of the other four subtle elements

For instance, the gross element Earth (Pṛthvī) is composed of:

- ❧ 1/2 of the subtle element Earth

- ❧ 1/8 of the subtle element Water

- ❧ 1/8 of the subtle element Fire

- ❧ 1/8 of the subtle element Air

- ❧ 1/8 of the subtle element Space

Significance

This process explains how the diverse physical world with its varied forms and properties is derived from the same five fundamental elements. It also highlights the interconnectedness and interdependence of all elements in the universe. Pañcīkaraṇam is an important concept in understanding the nature of the physical reality in Vedanta philosophy.

Composition of the Gross Element Earth (Pṛthvī)

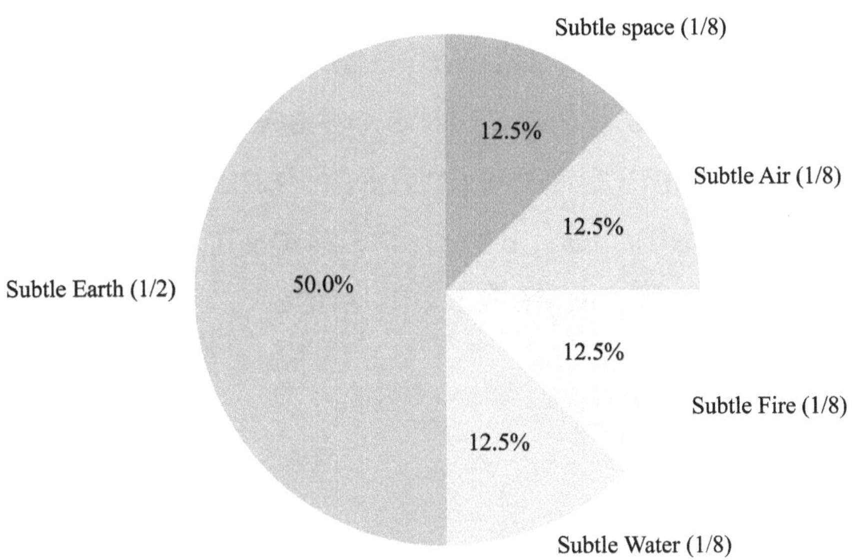

"

The Self is always present and
radiant, yet seems concealed by
ignorance. When ignorance is
removed, the Self shines forth
in its full brilliance.

"

Like waves that arise from and
dissolve into the ocean, the worlds
emerge from, exist within, and
return to Brahman.

पंचप्राणमनोबुद्धिदशेन्द्रियसमन्वितम् ।
अपंचीकृतभूतोत्थं सूक्ष्माङ्गं भोगसाधनम् ॥

pañcaprāṇamanobuddhidaśendriyasamanvitam ।
apañcīkṛtabhūtottham sūkṣmāṅgam bhogasādhanam ॥

पञ्चप्राण (pañcaprāṇa): the five vital airs; मनो (mano): mind; बुद्धि (buddhi): intellect; दशेन्द्रिय (daśendriya): the ten senses; समन्वितम् (samanvitam): endowed with; अपञ्चीकृत (apañcīkṛta): unsubtle, uncombined; भूतोत्थम् (bhūtottham): arising from the elements; सूक्ष्माङ्गम् (sūkṣmāṅgam): subtle body; भोगसाधनम् (bhogasādhanam): instrument of experience.

> **The subtle body consists of the five vital airs, mind, intellect, and ten senses. It is formed from the subtle elements and is the means for experiencing pleasure and pain.**

This verse explains the concept of the subtle body (sūkṣmāṅga) in Vedanta, distinct from the gross physical body and composed of refined elements. It includes the five vital airs (pañca-prāṇa) — prāṇa, apāna, vyāna, udāna, and samāna — which sustain life and govern physiological functions like circulation and digestion.

The subtle body also contains the mind (manas) and intellect (buddhi), responsible for sensory processing, emotions, reasoning, and decision-making, forming the core of cognitive and emotional experiences. Additionally, it houses the ten senses (daśendriya): the five sensory organs (jñānendriyas) for perception and the five motor organs (karmendriyas) for action.

The subtle body is "apañcīkṛta-bhūtottham," meaning it arises from the subtle essences (tanmātras) of the five elements before they form gross matter. It is described as "bhoga-sādhanam," the instrument of experience, through which the jīva-ātma interacts with and experiences the material world, mediating between the Self and physical existence.

～

अनाद्यविद्याऽनिर्वाच्या कारणोपाधिरुच्यते ।
उपाधित्रितयादन्यमात्मानमवधारयेत् ॥

anādyavidyā'nirvācyā kāraṇopādhirucyate |
upādhitritayādanyamātmānamavadhārayet ॥

अनादि (anādi): beginningless; अविद्या (avidyā): ignorance; अनिर्वाच्या (anirvācyā): indescribable; कारण (kāraṇa): causal; उपाधि (upādhi): limiting adjunct; उच्यते (ucyate): is called; उपाधि (upādhi): limiting adjunct; त्रितयात् (tritayāt): from the triad; अन्यम् (anyam): different; आत्मानम् (Ātmānam): the Self; अवधारयेत् (avadhārayet): should be understood.

The beginningless, indescribable avidya (ignorance) is called the causal limiting adjunct (kāraṇa upadhi). One should understand the Self as different from this triad of limiting adjuncts.

This verse explores the concept of avidyā (ignorance) in Advaita Vedanta, describing it as "anādi" (beginningless), meaning ignorance has no starting point and has always obscured the true Self (Ātman). Avidyā is also termed "anirvācyā" (indescribable), highlighting its paradoxical nature—neither real nor unreal. It defies logical categorization, existing without clear definition.

Avidyā is referred to as the "kāraṇa upādhi" (causal limiting adjunct), the most subtle limitation that gives rise to other superimpositions, obscuring the infinite Self. The verse also mentions a "tritaya" (triad of upādhis), referring to the three bodies in Vedanta: causal body (kāraṇa śarīra), subtle body (sūkṣma śarīra), and gross body (sthūla śarīra).

The key teaching of this verse is "Ātmānam-avadhārayet," meaning one should understand the Self as distinct from these limiting adjuncts. Advaita Vedanta asserts that the true Self (Ātman) is not bound by these limitations, including ignorance, leading to the realization of one's true, limitless nature.

∽

15

पंचकोशादियोगेन तत्तन्मय इव स्थितः ।
शुद्धात्मा नीलवस्त्रादियोगेन स्फटिको यथा ॥

pañcakośādiyogena tattanmaya iva sthitaḥ ।
śuddhātmā nīlavatrādiyogena sphaṭiko yathā ॥

पञ्चकोश-आदि-योगेन (pañcakośa ādi yogena): due to the association with the five sheaths; तत् (tat): that; तन्मय (tanmaya): identified with; इव (iva): as if; स्थितः (sthitaḥ): remains; शुद्धात्मा (śuddhĀtmā): the pure Self; नीलवस्त्र-आदि-योगेन (nīlavatra ādi yogena): due to the association with blue cloth; स्फटिकः (sphaṭikaḥ): crystal; यथा (yathā): just as.

> **Due to the association with the five sheaths, the pure Self appears as if identified with them, just as a crystal appears blue due to the association with a blue cloth.**

This verse delves into the concept of the pure Self (Ātma) and its apparent identification with the five sheaths (pañcakośa) in Advaita Vedanta. The five sheaths are layers covering the true Self, creating an illusion of individuality.

The annamaya kośa is the physical body nourished by food, while the prāṇamaya kośa is the vital energy sustaining life. The manomaya kośa governs the mind and emotions, the vijñānamaya kośa represents intellect and discernment, and the ānandamaya kośa reflects bliss experienced in deep sleep.

The verse explains that the pure Self (śuddhātma) appears identified with these sheaths due to ignorance (avidyā), but this identification is illusory. The Self remains pure and unaffected by these coverings.

The analogy of a crystal (sphaṭikaḥ) placed near a blue cloth (nīlavatra) illustrates this: the crystal appears blue but remains clear. Similarly, the Self appears associated with the sheaths but stays unchanged.

～

"

While knowledge is essential for the removal of ignorance, it is ultimately a means to an end. The goal is to reach a state of pure, unconditioned awareness where the distinctions created by the mind are transcended.

"

"

Look beyond the apparent reality
of the phenomenal world and to
awaken to the ultimate truth of
non-duality. The attachments and
aversions that dominate our worldly
life are part of an illusory experience.
True understanding and liberation
come from recognizing the ephemeral
nature of these experiences and
realizing the eternal, unchanging
reality of the Self.

16

वपुस्तुषादिभिः कोशैर्युक्तं युक्त्यवघाततः ।
आत्मानमन्तरं शुद्धं विविच्यात्तण्डुलं यथा ॥

vapustuṣādibhiḥ kośairyuktaṃ yuktyavaghātataḥ ।
Ātmānamantaraṃ śuddhaṃ vivicyāttaṇḍulaṃ yathā ॥

वपुः तुष आदिभिः (vapuḥ tuṣa ādi bhiḥ): with the body, husks and so forth; कोशैः (kośaiḥ): with sheaths; युक्तम् (yuktam): associated; युक्ति अवघाततः (yukti avaghātataḥ) by logical analysis and discrimination; आत्मानम् (Ātmānam): the Self; अन्तरम् (antaram): inner; शुद्धम् (śuddham): pure; विविच्यात् (vivicyāt): should be separated; तण्डुलम् (taṇḍulam): rice grain; यथा (yathā): just as.

> **One should distinguish the pure inner Self from the body and other sheaths through careful reasoning, just as rice is separated from its husk and other coverings.**

This verse compares the process of realizing the true Self (Ātma) to separating a rice grain from its husks. As mentioned in the earlier verse, Vedanta explains that the body is associated with five coverings or sheaths (kośas): annamaya (food sheath), prāṇamaya (vital air), manomaya (mental), vijñānamaya (intellectual), and ānandamaya (bliss). These sheaths obscure the true Self, much like husks cover a rice grain.

The verse advises using logical analysis and discrimination to separate the pure Self from these layers, just as one removes husks from rice.

This analogy highlights three points: the Self is distinct from its coverings, Self-realization requires effort and discrimination, and the true Self, once revealed, is pure and untouched.

~

17

सदा सर्वगतोऽप्यात्मा न सर्वत्रावभासते ।
बुद्धावेवावभासेत स्वच्छेषु प्रतिबिम्बवत् ॥

sadā sarvagato'pyātmā na sarvatrāvabhāsate ।
buddhāvevābhāsate svaccheṣu pratibimbavat ॥

सदा (sadā): always; सर्वगतः (sarvagataḥ): all-pervading; अपि (api): even though; आत्मा (Ātmā): the Self; न (na): not; सर्वत्र (sarvatra): everywhere; अवभासते (avabhāsate): manifests, appears; बुद्धौ (buddhau): in the intellect; एव (eva): alone; अवभासेत (avabhāsate): shines; स्वच्छेषु (svaccheṣu): in the pure; प्रतिबिम्बवत् (pratibimbavat): like a reflection.

Although the Self is always all-pervading, it does not manifest everywhere. It shines only in the intellect, just as a reflection appears only in a clear surface.

The Self is described as "sarvagataḥ," meaning omnipresent, existing everywhere. However, it does not manifest in all places, becoming apparent only in a pure and clear intellect (buddhi). The verse uses the analogy of a reflection (pratibimbavat) to illustrate this: just as a reflection is visible only on a clean, clear surface, the Self is perceived only in a mind free from desires, distractions, and impurities.

This emphasizes the need for mental purification and clarity for Self-realization. Although the Self is ever-present, it requires a purified and focused intellect as the medium for its recognition and understanding.

~

18

देहेन्द्रियमनोबुद्धिप्रकृतिभ्यो विलक्षणम् ।
तद्वृत्तिसाक्षिणं विद्यादात्मानं राजवत्सदा ॥

dehendriya-mano-buddhi-prakṛtibhyo vilakṣaṇam ।
tad-vṛtti-sākṣiṇaṁ vidyād-ātmānaṁ rājavat-sadā ॥

देह (deha): body; इन्द्रिय (indriya): senses; मनः (manaḥ): mind; बुद्धि (buddhi): intellect; प्रकृतिभ्यः (prakṛtibhyaḥ): from the nature; विलक्षणम् (vilakṣaṇam): distinct, different; तत् (tat): their; वृत्ति (vṛtti): activities, functions; साक्षिणम् (sākṣiṇam): witness; विद्यात् (vidyāt): should know; आत्मानम् (Ātmānam): the Self; राजवत् (rājavat): like a king; सदा (sadā): always.

> **Always understand the Self as different from the body, senses, mind, intellect, and nature. Know it to be the witness of their activities, just like a king (observes).**

This verse explains the nature of the Self (Ātma) and its relationship to the body and mind, highlighting that the Self is fundamentally separate from these entities. The Self is distinct from the body (deha), senses (indriya), mind (manaḥ), intellect (buddhi), and inherent nature (prakṛti). These components, often mistaken for the Self, are simply tools through which we engage with the world, but they do not represent the true essence of an individual. The Self transcends these temporary physical and mental faculties, remaining unaffected by their functions.

The verse further describes the Self as the eternal witness (sākṣi), quietly observing the activities of the body, senses, and mind without being influenced by them, much like a king watching his subjects. This analogy highlights the Self's detached nature, untouched by external or internal changes.

19

व्यापृतेष्विन्द्रियेष्वात्मा व्यापारीवाविवेकिनाम् ।
दृश्यतेऽभ्रेषु धावत्सु धावन्निव यथा शशी ॥

vyāpṛteṣvindriyeṣv-ātmā vyāpārīvāvivekinām ।
dṛśyate'bhreṣu dhāvatsu dhāvanniva yathā śaśī ॥

व्यापृतेषु (vyāpṛteṣu): when engaged; इन्द्रियेषु (indriyeṣu): in the senses; आत्मा (Ātmā): the Self; व्यापारी (vyāpārī): as an active agent; इव (iva): as if; अविवेकिनाम् (avivekinām): to the undiscerning; दृश्यते (dṛśyate): appears; अभ्रेषु (abhreṣu): among the clouds; धावत्सु (dhāvatsu): when moving; धावन् (dhāvann): moving; इव (iva): as if; यथा (yathā): like; शशी (śaśī): the moon.

> **When the senses are absorbed in external objects, the Self (Ātman) appears as though it is active and restless, much like the moon seems to move when clouds race across the sky.**

This verse uses an analogy to explain how the Self (Ātma) is understood by those who lack discernment (avivekinām). The senses (indriyās) are constantly engaged in various activities, and to those who do not have the wisdom to differentiate between the Self and the senses, it appears as if the Self is the one performing these actions.

The analogy used here is that of the moon (śaśī) and the clouds (abhreṣu). When clouds move across the sky, it can sometimes seem as if the moon is moving along with them. However, it is only the movement of the clouds that creates the illusion of motion of the moon. Similarly, the Self is ever-still and unchanging, but the movement and activities of the senses create the illusion that the Self is active and engaged in these activities.

20

आत्मचैतन्यमाश्रित्य देहेन्द्रियमनोधियः ।
स्वक्रियार्थेषु वर्तन्ते सूर्यालोकं यथा जनाः ॥

Ātma-caitanyam-āśritya dehendriya-mano-dhiyaḥ |
sva-kriyārtheṣu vartante sūryālokaṁ yathā janāḥ ||

आत्म (Ātma): Self; चैतन्यम् (caitanyam): consciousness; आश्रित्य (āśritya): depending on; देह (deha): body; इन्द्रिय (indriya): senses; मनः (manaḥ): mind; धियः (dhiyaḥ): intellect; स्व (sva): their own; क्रिया (kriyā): actions; अर्थेषु (artheṣu): for the purposes; वर्तन्ते (vartante): function; सूर्य (sūrya): Sun; आलोकम् (ālokam): light; यथा (yathā): just as; जनाः (janāḥ): people.

The body, senses, mind, and intellect perform their functions by relying on the consciousness of the Self, just as people carry out their activities in sunlight.

This verse highlights the relationship between the Self (Ātma) and the body-mind complex, emphasizing that the functions of the body (deha), senses (indriya), mind (manaḥ), and intellect (dhiyaḥ) are made possible by the underlying consciousness of the Self (Ātma-caitanyam).

The verse uses the analogy of the Sun (Sūrya) and its light (ālokam): just as people carry out their activities depending on the Sun's light, the body, senses, mind, and intellect function by relying on the consciousness of the Self. The Sun does not directly engage in people's activities, yet its light is essential. Similarly, the Self remains a passive witness, not engaging in actions, but its consciousness is vital for the functioning of the body-mind complex.

Understanding this distinction reveals the true nature of the Self as separate from the transient physical and mental faculties, helping one recognize the Self as the unchanging, illuminating force behind all bodily and mental functions.

~

"

Brahman is the only true reality.
All forms, names, and experiences
that seem to constitute the world are
merely superimpositions upon
this one indivisible reality. Until one
realizes Brahman through knowledge
and inner awakening, the world will
continue to deceive with its seeming
multiplicity and diversity.

"

Realize that the ultimate truth lies
in the substratum, rather than in the
fleeting phenomena of the universe.
Through this understanding, the
verse subtly encourages a shift in
focus from the transient to the
eternal, leading to liberation from
the cycle of birth and death.

21

देहेन्द्रियगुणान्कर्माण्यमले सच्चिदात्मनि ।
अध्यस्यन्त्यविवेकेन गगने नीलतादिवत् ॥

dehendriya-guṇān karmāṇy-amale saccidātmani ।
adhyasyanty-avivekena gagane nīlatādivat ॥

देह (deha): body; इन्द्रिय (indriya): senses; गुणान् (guṇān): qualities; कर्माणि (karmāṇi): actions; अमले (amale): pure; सच्चिदात्मनि (saccidātmani): in the existence-consciousness-Self; अध्यस्यन्ति (adhyasyanti): superimpose; अविवेकेन (avivekena): through ignorance; गगने (gagane): in the sky; नीलता (nīlatā): blueness; आदि (ādi): similar qualities; वत् (vat): as (possessing).

> **Due to ignorance, people wrongly attribute the qualities and actions of the body and senses to the pure Self (which is existence-consciousness), just as the colorless sky appears blue.**

This verse explains the concept of superimposition (adhyāsa) and how ignorance (aviveka) causes the mistaken identification of the Self with the body and senses. The Self (saccidātmani), which is pure existence-consciousness, is free from attributes and actions, yet ignorance leads people to superimpose the qualities (guṇān) and actions (karmāṇi) of the body and senses onto the Self.

The analogy of the sky (gagana) and its apparent blueness (nīlatā) illustrates this concept: just as the sky appears blue due to atmospheric conditions but is actually colorless, the Self remains pure and unaffected but seems to possess the qualities of the body due to ignorance.

This false identification creates a sense of individuality tied to the body and mind. Gaining discernment (viveka) allows one to remove ignorance and recognize the true, unchanging nature of the Self, free from all superimpositions, leading to the realization of true knowledge (jñāna).

~

22

अज्ञानान्मानसोपाधेः कर्तृत्वादीनि चात्मनि ।
कल्प्यन्तेऽम्बुगते चन्द्रे चलनादि यथाम्भसः ॥

ajñānān mānasopādheḥ kartṛtvādīni cātmai ।
kalpyante'mbugate candre calanādi yathāmbhasaḥ ॥

अज्ञानात् (ajñānāt): due to ignorance; मानस (mānasa): of the mind; उपाधेः (upādheḥ): limiting adjunct; कर्तृत्व (kartṛtva): doership; आदीनि (ādīni): etc.; च (ca): and; आत्मनि (Ātmai): in the Self; कल्प्यन्ते (kalpyante): are imagined; अम्बु (ambu): water; गते (gate): present; चन्द्रे (candre): in the moon; चलन (calana): movement; आदि (ādi): etc.; यथा (yathā): as; अम्भसः (ambhasaḥ): in the water.

Due to ignorance and the limitations of the mind, qualities like doership are imagined in the Self, just as motion is falsely attributed to the moon reflected in water.

This verse explains how ignorance (ajñāna) causes the false identification of the Self (Ātma) with the mind and its attributes, using the analogy of the moon reflected in water. The Self, inherently pure and unchanging, becomes superimposed with qualities like doership due to ignorance, much like how the reflection of the moon in water appears to move or distort, though the moon itself remains unaffected.

Just as the moon is unaffected by the reflection's movement, the Self is unaffected by the mind's activities. The attributes attributed to the Self are mere illusions created by the mind, similar to the illusory qualities in the moon's reflection.

The verse emphasizes the importance of discernment (viveka) to recognize the distinction between the true Self and the illusory attributes imposed by the mind, leading to a clearer understanding of the Self's unchanging nature.

~

23

रागेच्छासुखदुःखादि बुद्धौ सत्यां प्रवर्तते ।
सुषुप्तौ नास्ति तन्नाशे तस्माद्बुद्धेस्तु नात्मनः ॥

rāgecchā-sukha-duḥkhādi buddhau satyāṁ pravartate ।
suṣuptau nāsti tannāśe tasmād buddhes tu nātmānaḥ ॥

राग (rāga): attachment; इच्छा (icchā): desire; सुख (sukha): pleasure; दुःख (duḥkha): pain; आदि (ādi): and so on; बुद्धौ (buddhau): in the intellect; सत्याम् (satyām): when present; प्रवर्तते (pravartate): arise; सुषुप्तौ (suṣuptau): in deep sleep; नास्ति (nāsti): do not exist; तत् (tat): they; नाशे (nāśe): in absence; तस्मात् (tasmāt): therefore; बुद्धेः (buddheḥ): of the intellect; तु (tu): but; न (na): not; आत्मनः (Ātmanaḥ): of the Self.

Things like attachment, desire, happiness, and sorrow appear when the mind is active. They disappear in deep sleep when the mind is inactive. So, these belong to the mind, not to our true Self.

This verse highlights the distinction between the Self (Ātma) and the intellect (buddhi), showing that emotional and mental states such as attachment (rāga), desire (icchā), pleasure (sukha), and pain (duḥkha) are functions of the intellect, not the Self. The Self is pure consciousness, unaffected by the states experienced by the intellect.

When the intellect is active, these emotions and mental states arise, but during deep sleep (suṣupti), when the intellect is inactive, these states do not exist. This absence of attachment, desire, pleasure, and pain during deep sleep demonstrates that they are attributes of the intellect, not the Self.

The verse underscores that the Self is distinct from the intellect, with mental states being superimpositions that arise from the intellect's activities. Thus, the Self remains pure, unchanging, and untouched by these temporary states of mind.

~

24

प्रकाशोऽर्कस्य तोयस्य शैत्यमग्रेर्यथोष्णता ।
स्वभावः सच्चिदानन्दनित्यनिर्मलतात्मनः ॥

prakāśo'arkasya toyasya śaityamagner yathoṣṇatā ।
svabhāvaḥ saccidānanda-nitya-nirmalatātmaah ॥

प्रकाशः (prakāśaḥ): light; अर्कस्य (arkasya): of the Sun; तोयस्य (toyasya): of water; शैत्यम् (śaityam): coolness; अग्रेः (agner): of fire; यथा (yathā): just as; उष्णता (uṣṇatā): heat; स्वभावः (svabhāvaḥ): nature; सत्-चित्-आनन्द (sat-cit-ānanda): existence-consciousness-bliss; नित्य (nitya): eternal; निर्मलता (nirmalatā): purity; आत्मनः (Ātmaah): of the Self.

> **Just as light is the nature of the Sun, coolness of water, and heat of fire, so existence-consciousness-bliss and eternal purity are the nature of the Self.**

This verse illustrates the intrinsic nature of the Self (Ātma) through analogies from nature, comparing the Self's essential qualities to those of the Sun, water, and fire. Just as light is inherent to the Sun, coolness to water, and heat to fire, existence-consciousness-bliss (sat-cit-ānanda) is the inherent nature of the Self. These qualities are not temporary but are integral to the Self's essence.

The Self is described as eternal (nitya) and pure (nirmala), unchanging and free from impurities. Sat (existence) signifies that the Self is the ultimate reality, Chit (consciousness) denotes it as the source of all awareness, and Ananda (bliss) reflects it as the source of ultimate happiness. These qualities are inseparable from the Self, just as light, coolness, and heat are inseparable from their respective elements.

Recognizing these intrinsic qualities helps one distinguish the eternal Self from the transient and changing attributes of the body and mind, aiding in understanding the true nature of the Self.

25

आत्मनः सच्चिदंशश्च बुद्धेर्वृत्तिरिति द्वयम् ।
संयोज्य चाविवेकेन जानामीति प्रवर्तते ॥

Ātmānaḥ saccidaṁśaś ca buddher vṛttir iti dvayam ।
saṁyojya cāvivekena jānāmīti pravartate ॥

आत्मनः (Ātmanah): of the Self; सत्-चित्-अंशः (sat-cit-aṁśaḥ): the aspect of existence-consciousness; च (ca): and; बुद्धेः (buddheḥ): of the intellect; वृत्तिः (vṛttiḥ): function, modification; इति (iti): thus; द्वयम् (dvayam): the two; संयोज्य (saṁyojya): combining; च (ca): and; अविवेकेन (avivekena): through non-discrimination; जानामि (jānāmi): I know; इति (iti): thus; प्रवर्तते (pravartate): functions, operates.

> **The 'I know' experience happens when we mistakenly mix up two things: the unchanging awareness that is our true Self, and the changing thoughts in our mind.**

This verse explains how the sense of individual doer-ship arises from the mistaken identification of the Self (Ātma) with the intellect (buddhi). The Self, characterized by pure existence-consciousness (sat-chit), is awareness without action, while the intellect undergoes modifications responsible for thoughts and actions.

When the Ātma and buddhi are confused due to lack of discernment (aviveka), the egoistic assertion "I know" emerges, leading to the false belief that the Self is performing actions. This identification (of the Ātma) with the intellect causes the experience of individuality and doership, though these are products of the intellect, not the Self.

The verse stresses the need for discernment (viveka) to distinguish between the Self and the intellect. By developing this clarity, one can recognize the Self as unchanging awareness, free from the intellect's modifications, and thus transcend the ego, achieving Self-knowledge (jñāna).

~

"

While the world appears to be full
of diverse forms, these forms are
ultimately unreal when seen in the
light of true knowledge. They are
mere appearances on the substratum
of the eternal, all-pervading
consciousness that is Vishnu
or Brahman.

"

"

The realization that all diversity is
merely an appearance, and that
in essence there is only the one,
non-dual reality, is considered the
highest spiritual knowledge leading
to liberation (mokṣa).

26

आत्मनो विक्रिया नास्ति बुद्धेर्बोधो न जात्विति ।
जीवः सर्वमलं ज्ञात्वा ज्ञाता द्रष्टेति मुह्यति ॥

Ātmano vikriyā nāsti buddher bodho na jātv iti ।
jīvaḥ sarvam alaṁ jñātvā jñātā draṣṭeti muhyati ॥

आत्मनः (Ātmanah): of the Self; विक्रिया (vikriyā): change; नास्ति (nāsti): does not exist; बुद्धेः (buddheh): of the intellect; बोधः (bodhah): consciousness; न (na): not; जातु (jātu): ever; इति (iti): thus; जीवः (Jvīvah): the individual soul; सर्वम् (sarvam): everything; अलम् (alam): fully; ज्ञात्वा (jñātvā): knowing; ज्ञाता (jñātā): the knower; द्रष्टा (draṣṭā): the seer; इति (iti): thus; मुह्यति (muhyati): gets deluded.

The true Self never changes, and the mind itself can't really know anything (by itself). But the individual person gets confused and thinks 'I am the one who knows' and 'I am the one who sees'.

This verse explains the relationship between the Self (Ātma), intellect (buddhi), and the delusion experienced by the individual soul (jīva). The Self is pure, unchanging consciousness, while the intellect processes thoughts and experiences but is not inherently conscious. The intellect only appears conscious by reflecting the light of the Self, much like the moon reflects the light of the Sun.

Due to ignorance (avidyā), the jīva mistakenly identifies the intellect's functions with the Self, leading to the false belief that the Self is the doer (kartā) and experiencer (bhoktā). This creates the illusion of individuality and separation. The intellect causes the jīva to believe "I am the knower" (jñātā) and "I am the seer" (draṣṭā), resulting in delusion.

Through discernment (viveka), one can distinguish between the unchanging Self and the intellect's changing functions, realizing the Self as the eternal, unchanging witness of all experiences, beyond the intellect's activities.

27

रज्जुसर्पवदात्मानं जीवं ज्ञात्वा भयं वहेत् ।
नाहं जीवः परात्मेति ज्ञातं चेन्निर्भयो भवेत् ॥

rajju-sarpa-vat ātmānaṁ jīvaṁ jñātvā bhayaṁ vahet ।
nāhaṁ jīvaḥ parātmeti jñātaṁ cen nirbhayo bhavet ॥

रज्जु (rajju): rope; सर्पवत् (sarpa-vat): like a snake; आत्मानम् (Ātmānam): the Self; जीवम् (Jīvam): individual Self; ज्ञात्वा (jñātvā): knowing; भयम् (bhayam): fear; वहेत् (vahet): would experience; न (na): not; अहम् (aham): I; जीवः (jīvaḥ): individual soul; पर (para): Supreme; आत्मा (Ātmā): Self; इति (iti): thus; ज्ञातम् (jñātam): known; चेत् (cet): if; निर्भयः (nirbhayaḥ): fearless; भवेत् (bhavet): would become.

Just as a rope mistaken for a snake causes fear, the Ātman (Self) is mistaken for the jīva (individual soul), leading to fear. But when one realizes, "I am not the jīva, I am the Supreme Self," all delusion disappears, and fear vanishes.

The analogy of mistaking a rope for a snake is used to illustrate how fear and delusion arise from ignorance. Just as fear occurs when a rope is misperceived as a snake, fear and suffering arise when the Self, which is pure consciousness and the Supreme Reality, is mistakenly identified as the ego-self with a sense of agency. This mistaken identity causes fear because the limited Self is subject to birth, death, and limitations.

However, when one realizes, "I am not the ego-self, but the Supreme Self," this correct understanding dispels ignorance and reveals the Self's true nature as infinite and eternal. This realization brings a state of fearlessness, as the Self is beyond all limitations.

Recognizing the Self as the Supreme Reality (para-ātma) allows one to transcend the dualities and fears associated with individual existence. Discernment and Self-knowledge are the keys to overcoming delusion, leading to liberation and fearlessness.

~

आत्मावभासयत्येको बुद्ध्यादीनीन्द्रियाण्यपि ।
दीपो घटादिवत्स्वात्मा जडैस्तैर्नावभास्यते ॥

Ātmāvabhāsayaty eko buddhy-ādīnīndriyāṇy api ।
dīpo ghaṭādivat svātmā jaḍais tair nāvabhāsyate ॥

आत्मा (Ātmā): the Self; अवभासयति (avabhāsayati): illumines; एकः (ekaḥ): alone; बुद्धि-आदीनि (buddhi-ādīni): intellect and others; इन्द्रियाणि (indriyāṇi): senses; अपि (api): even; दीपः (dīpaḥ): lamp; घट-आदिवत् (ghaṭa-ādivat): like a pot and so forth; स्वात्मा (svātmā): own Self; जडैः (jaḍaiḥ): by the inert; तैः (taiḥ): by them; न (na): not; अवभास्यते (avabhāsyate): illumined.

> **The Self lights up the mind and senses,
> like a lamp lights up objects around it.
> But just as those objects can't light up
> the lamp, the mind and senses can't
> illuminate the Self.**

This verse highlights the illuminating nature of the Self (Ātma) and its relationship with the intellect (buddhi) and senses (indriyāṇi). The Self is compared to a lamp that illuminates objects like pots, signifying that it provides the light of consciousness that enables the intellect and senses to function.

The Self is the sole source of awareness, allowing the mind and senses to perceive the world, but it remains pure and unchanging. The intellect and senses, like inert objects, cannot function on their own; they are non-conscious and rely on the Self's illumination to operate.

However, the Self does not depend on these entities for its light, just as a lamp does not need the objects it illuminates. This realization reveals the Self as the independent and Self-sufficient source of consciousness, separate from the mind-body complex.

Understanding this distinction leads to deeper Self-awareness and recognition of the Self as the ultimate essence of existence.

29

स्वबोधे नान्यबोधेच्छा बोधरूपतयात्मनः ।
न दीपस्यान्यदीपेच्छा यथा स्वात्मप्रकाशने ॥

svabodhe nānyabodhecchā bodharūpatayātmānaḥ ।
na dīpasyānyadīpecchā yathā svātma-prakāśane ॥

स्वबोधे (svabodhe): for its discovery; न (na): not; अन्यबोधेच्छा (anyabodhecchā): need for another source of knowledge; बोधरूपतया (bodharūpatayā): due to being of the nature of consciousness; आत्मनः (Ātmānaḥ): of the Self; न (na): not; दीपस्य (dīpasya): of a lamp; अन्यदीपेच्छा (anyadīpecchā): need for another lamp; यथा (yathā): just as; स्वात्मप्रकाशने (svātma-prakāśane): in illuminating itself.

> **To know your true Self, you don't need any other knowledge, because your true Self is knowledge itself. It's like how a lamp doesn't need another lamp to shine its own light.**

This verse emphasizes the Self-illumining nature of the Self (Ātma). The Self is inherently of the nature of consciousness, meaning it is Self-aware and does not require an external source to illuminate or make it known. This idea is illustrated using the analogy of a lamp.

The Self, being pure consciousness, is Self-evident. It does not need another form of knowledge or awareness to make it known, just as a lamp does not need another lamp to reveal its light. The lamp naturally illuminates itself and its surroundings by its very nature.

This verse serves as a reminder that the pursuit of Self-knowledge is about uncovering what is already present and Self-evident. By realizing that the Self is inherently luminous and independent of external supports, one can achieve a deeper understanding and experience of one's true nature.

~

30

निषिध्य निखिलोपाधीन्नेति नेतीति वाक्यतः ।
विद्यादैक्यं महावाक्यैर्जीवात्मपरमात्मनोः ॥

niṣidhya nikhilopādhīn neti netīti vākyataḥ ।
vidyād aikyaṁ mahāvākyair jīvātma-paramātmaoḥ ॥

निषिध्य (niṣidhya): negating; निखिल-उपाधीन् (nikhila-upādhīn): all limiting adjuncts; नेति नेति (neti neti): "not this, not this"; इति (iti): thus; वाक्यतः (vākyataḥ): through the statements; विद्यात् (vidyāt): should know; ऐक्यम् (aikyam): oneness; महावाक्यैः (mahāvākyaiḥ): through the great sayings; जीवात्म-परमात्मनोः (jīvātma-paramātmanoḥ): of the individual Self and the Supreme Self.

> **By rejecting all limitations using the teaching 'not this, not this', one should realize the oneness of the jīvātma and the paramātma through the great Vedantic statements.**

This verse explains the method of realizing the true nature of the Self through the process of negation (neti neti) and the teachings of the Mahavakyas. "Neti neti" means "not this, not this" and involves negating all limiting adjuncts (upādhīs) such as the body, mind, and senses, which are mistakenly identified as the Self.

By continuously negating these adjuncts, one discards false identifications and uncovers the true, infinite Self. The verse also highlights the significance of the mahāvākyas, great sayings from the Upanishads, such as "tat tvam asi" (that thou art) and "Aham Brahmasmi" (I am Brahman), which declare the oneness of the individual soul (jīvātma) and the Supreme Self (paramātma).

~

"

The Self, which is pure existence-
consciousness, is free from attributes
and actions, yet ignorance leads
people to superimpose the qualities
and actions of the body and
senses onto the Self.

"

In Vedanta, understanding the
nature of the subtle body is crucial for
Self-discovery. It helps in recognizing
that the true Self (Ātmā) is beyond
both the gross and subtle bodies,
leading to the realization of one's true
nature as pure consciousness, free
from the limitations of the physical
and subtle bodies. This realization
is essential for attaining liberation
(mokṣa) and transcending the cycle
of birth and death.

31

आविद्यकं शरीरादि दृश्यं बुद्बुदवत्क्षरम् ।
एतद्विलक्षणं विद्यादहं ब्रह्मेति निर्मलम् ॥

āvidyakaṁ śarīrādi dṛśyaṁ budbudavat kṣaram ।
etad vilakṣaṇaṁ vidyād ahaṁ brahmeti nirmalam ॥

आविद्यकम् (āvidyakam): born of ignorance; शरीरादि (śarīrādi): body, etc.; दृश्यम् (dṛśyam): the visible; बुद्बुदवत् (budbudavat): like a bubble; क्षरम् (kṣaram): perishable; एतत् (etat): this; विलक्षणम् (vilakṣaṇam): distinct; विद्यात् (vidyāt): should know; अहम् (aham): I; ब्रह्म (brahma): Brahman, the Absolute; इति (iti): thus; निर्मलम् (nirmalam): untainted.

> **The body and everything we see are products of ignorance and are as temporary as bubbles. You should understand that you are different from all this - you are the pure, eternal Self.**

This verse, like the previous one, emphasizes the distinction between the transient physical body and the eternal, pure Self (Ātma). The body and its attributes, born from ignorance (avidya), are subject to the limitations, imperfections, and impermanence of the material world, much like fragile bubbles that easily burst. These physical forms are visible to the senses but are temporary and ever-changing.

In contrast, the true Self is unchanging, unaffected by the body's decay. Recognizing this distinction leads one to realize their true nature as Brahman (aham brahma), the infinite, pure, and untainted reality (nirmalam). The verse encourages seekers to shift their identification from the temporary physical body to the eternal Self, which leads to liberation (mokṣa) and true knowledge (jñāna).

By internalizing the knowledge "I am Brahman," one transcends the limitations imposed by ignorance and realizes their eternal, unchanging essence, thereby attaining Self-realization and liberation from worldly delusion.

32

देहान्यत्वान्न मे जन्मजराकार्श्यलयादयः ।
शब्दादिविषयैः सङ्गो निरिन्द्रियतया न च ॥

dehānyatvān na me janma-jarā-kārśya-layādayaḥ ।
śabdādi-viṣayaiḥ saṅgo nirindriyatayā na ca ॥

देहान्यत्वात् (deha-anyatvāt): due to being other than the body; न (na): not; मे (me): to me; जन्म (janma): birth; जर (jarā): old age; कर्ष्य (kārśya): emaciation; लय (laya): death; आदयः (ādayaḥ): and so on; शब्द (śabda): sound; आदि (ādi): etc., and so on; विषयैः (viṣayaiḥ): with objects; सङ्गः (saṅgaḥ): contact; न (na): not; च (ca): and; निरिन्द्रियतया (nirindriyatayā): due to being without senses.

> **Since the Ātma (I am) is other than the body, birth, old age, emaciation, death, and such do not belong to me. Being without senses, I (the Ātma) have no contact with objects such as sound and so on.**

This verse highlights the distinction between the Self (Ātma) and the physical body, as well as the sensory experiences linked to it. The Self is described as eternal and unchanging, unaffected by the body's birth, aging, or death. The body and its attributes are products of ignorance (avidya) and subject to physical changes, but the Self remains untouched.

Additionally, the Self does not directly engage with sensory experiences like sound, sight, or touch, as these are functions of the body and mind. Understanding this distinction is crucial for Self-realization. By recognizing that the true Self is beyond physical and sensory experiences, one can detach from the body and mind, realizing their true nature as pure consciousness.

This realization leads to liberation (mokṣa) and freedom from duality (samsāra). By internalizing this knowledge, individuals can cultivate detachment from physical and mental limitations and focus on the eternal, unchanging nature of the Self.

33

अमनस्त्वान्न मे दुःखरागद्वेषभयादयः ।
अप्राणो ह्यमनाः शुभ्र इत्यादि श्रुतिशासनात् ॥

amanastvān na me duḥkha-rāga-dveṣa-bhayādayaḥ ।
aprāṇo hy amanāḥ śubhra ityādi śruti-śāsanāt ॥

अमनस्त्वात् (amanastvāt): due to being without mind; न (na): not; मे (me): to me; दुःख (duḥkha): sorrow; राग (rāga): attachment; द्वेष (dveṣa): aversion; भय (bhaya): fear; आदयः (ādayaḥ): and so on; अप्राणः (aprāṇaḥ): without vital airs (prana); हि (hi): indeed; अमनाः (amanāḥ): without mind; शुभ्र (śubhra): pure; इति (iti): thus; आदि (ādi): etc.; श्रुति (śruti): scriptural text; शासनात् (śāsanāt): instruction, teaching.

> **Because I am (the Self) beyond the mind, I do not experience sorrow, attachment, aversion, fear, or similar emotions. The scriptures declare, "The Self is without prāṇa, without mind, and pure."**

This verse highlights the distinction between the Self (Ātma) and the mind and vital functions, emphasizing that the Self is beyond mental and physical processes. Described as without mind (amanas) and without vital airs (aprāṇa), the Self is not affected by emotions like sorrow, attachment, aversion, or fear, which are attributes of the mind.

Since the Self is pure consciousness, it remains untouched by these mental afflictions. The verse also references scriptural teachings, which affirm that the Self is pure and transcends the realms of mind and body. By quoting these scriptures, the verse reinforces the idea that the Self is independent of physical and mental limitations.

~

34

निर्गुणो निष्क्रियो नित्यो निर्विकल्पो निरंजनः ।
निर्विकारो निराकारो नित्यमुक्तोऽस्मि निर्मलः ॥

nirguṇo niṣkriyo nityo nirvikalpo nirañjanaḥ ।
nirvikāro nirākāro nityamukto'smi nirmalaḥ ॥

निर्गुणः (nirguṇaḥ): without qualities; निष्क्रियः (niṣkriyaḥ): without action; नित्यः (nityaḥ): eternal; निर्विकल्पः (nirvikalpaḥ): without thought, undifferentiated; निरंजनः (nirañjanaḥ): without taint, pure; निर्विकारः (nirvikāraḥ): without change; निराकारः (nirākāraḥ): formless; नित्यमुक्तः (nityamuktaḥ): eternally free; अस्मि (asmi): I am; निर्मलः (nirmalaḥ): pure.

> **I am without qualities, without action, eternal, undifferentiated, pure, without change, formless, eternally free, and immaculate.**

This verse highlights the transcendental nature of the Self (Ātma) through a series of negations. The Self is described as "nirguṇaḥ," beyond all qualities, and "niṣkriyaḥ," free from actions, emphasizing that it is unaffected by the material world and its activities. The Self is also "nityaḥ," eternal, existing beyond time, and "nirvikalpaḥ," free from thoughts and dualities, signifying its pure, undifferentiated awareness.

Furthermore, the Self is "nirañjanaḥ," without impurities, and "nirvikāraḥ," unchanging, unaffected by the transient phenomena of the world. It is "nirākāraḥ," without form, transcending physical characteristics, and "nityamuktaḥ," inherently liberated, always free from the bondage of the material realm. Lastly, "nirmalaḥ" underscores the Self's spotless, pure nature.

This verse encourages the seeker to recognize the Self's eternal, unchanging, and pure essence, untouched by the limitations of the material and mental worlds, leading to a deeper understanding of true freedom.

~

35

अहमाकाशवत्सर्वं बहिरन्तर्गतोऽच्युतः ।
सदा सर्वसमः सिद्धो निःसङ्गो निर्मलोऽचलः ॥

aham ākāśavat sarvaṁ bahir antargato'cyutaḥ ।
sadā sarvasamaḥ siddho niḥsaṅgo nirmalo'calaḥ ॥

अहम् (aham): I; आकाशवत् (ākāśavat): like space; सर्वम् (sarvam): all; बहि: (bahiḥ): outside; अन्त: (antaḥ): inside; गत: (gataḥ): pervading; अच्युतः (acyutaḥ): imperishable; सदा (sadā): always; सर्वसमः (sarvasamaḥ): equal to all; सिद्धः (siddhaḥ): perfect, accomplished; निःसङ्गः (niḥsaṅgaḥ): unattached; निर्मलः (nirmalaḥ): pure; अचलः (acalaḥ): immovable.

I am like space, pervading everything inside and outside, imperishable, always equal to all, perfect, unattached, pure, and immovable.

This verse describes the Self (Ātma) as omnipresent and transcendental, like space (ākāśavat), which accommodates everything without being affected. Just as space remains untouched by what it holds, the Self pervades all existence, remaining untainted by worldly experiences and dualities, emphasizing that it transcends physical limitations and boundaries.

The Self exists both "inside" and "outside," signifying its omnipresence beyond any form or location. The term "acyuta," meaning imperishable, highlights the Self's eternal and unchanging nature. Unlike the transient physical world, subject to change and decay, the Self is constant, timeless, and indestructible.

Always equal, unattached, and pure, the Self remains unaffected by emotions, desires, and actions, maintaining a state of perfection and balance.

This verse encapsulates the Self as beyond physical limitations, embodying purity, perfection, and eternal presence.

~

"

By emphasizing the distinction between the Self and the upādhis, Advaita Vedanta points towards the path of Self-realization. It encourages the seeker to discriminate between what is truly the Self and what are merely limitations or coverings.

"

The apparent identification with the sheaths is due to ignorance, and through knowledge and discernment, one can realize the true nature of the Self. This realization is the essence of liberation (mokṣa), where one understands that the Self is pure consciousness, free from the limitations imposed by the sheaths.

नित्यशुद्धविमुक्तैकमखण्डानन्दमद्वयम् ।
सत्यं ज्ञानमनन्तं यत्परं ब्रह्माहमेव तत् ॥

nityaśuddhavimuktaikam akhaṇḍānandam advayam ।
satyaṁ jñānam anantaṁ yat paraṁ brahmāham eva tat ॥

नित्य (nitya): eternal; शुद्ध (śuddha): pure; विमुक्त (vimukta): free; एकम् (ekam): one; अखण्ड (akhaṇḍa): indivisible; आनन्दम् (ānandam): bliss; अद्वयम् (advayam): non-dual; सत्यम् (satyaṁ): truth; ज्ञानम् (jñānam): knowledge; अनन्तम् (anantaṁ): infinite; यत् (yat): which; परम् (param): supreme; ब्रह्म (brahma): Brahman; अहम् (aham): I; एव (eva): indeed; तत् (tat): that.

> **I am (the Ātma is) truly that ultimate reality which is always pure, completely free, one without a second, unbroken joy, non-dual, truth, knowledge, endless, and supreme.**

This verse describes various attributes of Brahman for the sake of discussion, even though Brahman is ultimately attributeless. Brahman's eternal nature means it exists beyond time and remains unaffected by birth and death, serving as the constant substratum of all that exists. Its purity indicates freedom from imperfection, untouched by the dualities of the material world.

Brahman's freedom reflects its unbounded nature, free from ignorance and suffering, representing the essence of liberation (mokṣa). Its oneness and indivisibility reinforce the non-dualistic view that all multiplicity is an illusion (māyā). Brahman embodies infinite bliss, unlike the fleeting pleasures of the material world, and realizing one's unity with Brahman leads to supreme bliss.

37

एवं निरन्तराभ्यस्ता ब्रह्मैवास्मीति वासना ।
हरत्यविद्याविक्षेपान् रोगानिव रसायनम् ॥

evaṃ nirantarābhyastā brahmaivāsmi iti vāsanā ।
haratyavidyāvikṣepān rogān iva rasāyanam ॥

एवम् (evaṃ): thus; निरन्तर (nirantara): continuous; अभ्यस्ता (abhyastā): practiced; ब्रह्म (brahma): Brahman; एव (eva): indeed; अस्मि (asmi): I am; इति (iti): thus; वासना (vāsanā): impression or thought; हरति (harati): removes; अविद्या (avidyā): ignorance; विक्षेपान् (vikṣepān): distractions; रोगान् (rogān): diseases; इव (iva): like; रसायनम् (rasāyanam): medicine or elixir.

Constantly meditating on the thought 'I am the ultimate reality (Brahman)' removes the confusions caused by ignorance, just as medicine cures diseases.

This verse highlights the transformative power of sustained meditation on one's identity with Brahman. It suggests that by continuously practicing the thought, "I am indeed Brahman," one can systematically remove the distractions, illusions, and ignorance that cloud the mind. This practice is likened to an elixir or powerful medicine that cures diseases, symbolizing the profound healing and purifying effects it has on the practitioner's consciousness.

The verse emphasizes that through deep and persistent contemplation of one's true nature as Brahman, the non-dual ultimate reality, one can dispel this ignorance and achieve a state of clarity and peace.

The metaphor of medicine curing disease illustrates how essential and effective this spiritual practice is for those seeking liberation. By cultivating a deep, unwavering conviction of one's identity with Brahman, the mind is transformed, the ego dissolves, and one attains the realization of their true Self.

~

38

विविक्तदेश आसीनो विरागो विजितेन्द्रियः ।
भावयेदेकमात्मानं तमनन्तमनन्यधीः ॥

viviktadeśa āsīno virāgo vijitendriyaḥ ।
bhāvayed ekam ātmānaṃ tam anantam ananyadhīḥ ॥

विविक्तदेश (viviktadeśa): in a secluded place; आसीनः (āsīnaḥ): sitting; विरागः (virāgaḥ): dispassionate; विजितेन्द्रियः (vijitendriyaḥ): having conquered the senses; भावयेत् (bhāvayet): should meditate; एकम् (ekam): one; आत्मानम् (Ātmānam): Self; तम् (tam): that; अनन्तम् (anantam): infinite; अनन्यधीः (ananyadhīḥ): with undistracted mind.

Sit in a quiet place, free from attachments, with your senses under control. Then, with undistracted attention, meditate on the one limitless Self.

This verse offers guidance on meditation for realizing one's true nature, emphasizing the importance of specific conditions and mental states for effective practice. Meditating in a secluded place, free from distractions, helps focus the mind inward and detach from external stimuli. This quiet setting allows the practitioner to concentrate fully on the inner Self without interference.

Dispassion, or virāga, is essential for renouncing worldly desires and emotional attachments, which cloud the mind and prevent deep meditation. By cultivating detachment, the practitioner can maintain mental clarity and transcend the fluctuations caused by desires and aversions.

Mastery over the senses, or vijitendriya, is crucial for avoiding distractions and achieving deeper levels of concentration and introspection.

This focused meditation ultimately leads to the realization of one's true nature as the infinite, non-dual Self, bringing the practitioner closer to true freedom.

～

39

आत्मन्येवाखिलं दृश्यं प्रविलाप्य धिया सुधीः ।
भावयेदेकमात्मानं निर्मलाकाशवत्सदा ॥

Ātmani evākhilaṃ dṛśyaṃ pravilāpya dhiyā sudhīḥ ।
bhāvayed ekam ātmānaṃ nirmalākāśavat sadā ॥

आत्मनि (Ātmani): in the Self; एव (eva): indeed; अखिलम् (akhilam): all; दृश्यम् (dṛśyam): the visible or perceivable; प्रविलाप्य (pravilāpya): having dissolved; धिया (dhiyā): with the intellect; सुधीः (sudhīḥ): the wise one; भावयेत् (bhāvayet): should meditate; एकम् (ekam): One; आत्मानम् (Ātmānam): Self; निर्मल (nirmala): pure; आकाशवत् (ākāśavat): like space; सदा (sadā): always.

> **A wise person should mentally dissolve everything they see into the Self, and constantly meditate on the one Self, which is as pure and vast as the clear sky.**

This verse guides the seeker in the practice of meditation for Self-realization, emphasizing the dissolution of all perceivable phenomena into the Self. It instructs the practitioner to see beyond the apparent multiplicity of the world and recognize that all phenomena are expressions of the same underlying reality—Brahman, which is identical to the Self (Ātma).

Using the intellect (dhiyā), the wise (sudhīḥ) are encouraged to engage in discernment, distinguishing the real from the unreal, leading to a deeper understanding of the Self as the only true existence. The verse compares the Self to space (ākāśa), vast and formless, unaffected by what it contains, symbolizing the infinite and pure nature of the Self.

By meditating on the Self as one and pure, the practitioner realizes their true nature and attains liberation (mokṣa). This practice dissolves the illusion of separateness and duality, revealing the unity of the Self as the ultimate reality.

~

40

रूपवर्णादिकं सर्वं विहाय परमार्थवित् ।
परिपूर्णचिदानन्दस्वरूपेणावतिष्ठते ॥

rūpavarṇādikaṃ sarvaṃ vihāya paramārthavit |
paripūrṇacidānandasvarūpeṇāvatiṣṭhate ॥

रूपवर्णादिकम् (rūpavarṇādikam): form, color, and so on; सर्वम् (sarvam): all; विहाय (vihāya): having abandoned; परमार्थवित् (paramārthavit): the knower of the supreme truth; परिपूर्ण (paripūrṇa): complete; चित् (cit): consciousness; आनन्द (ānanda): bliss; स्वरूपेण (svarūpeṇa): in the essence or nature; अवतिष्ठते (avatiṣṭhate): abides.

> **One who knows the highest truth lets go of all physical characteristics like form and color, and remains as pure, complete consciousness and bliss.**

This verse describes the state of a realized being who has attained knowledge of the supreme Truth, transcending external appearances and realizing their true nature. The phrase "having abandoned all forms, colors, and such" signifies detachment from the sensory world, where the seeker moves beyond superficial and transient aspects of existence like physical forms and perceptions.

The "knower of the supreme truth" refers to one who understands the non-dual nature of reality, recognizing the Self (Ātma) as identical with Brahman, the infinite, unchanging reality. Abiding "in the essence of complete consciousness and bliss" represents the state of enlightenment, where one experiences their true nature as pure consciousness and bliss.

This realization leads to a profound sense of completeness, free from the limitations and suffering of the material world. The verse emphasizes the transformative journey from identification with the body and mind to the realization of one's eternal, blissful essence.

"

Look beyond the superficial aspects
of existence to identify with the
deeper, unchanging reality of the
Self. This understanding is essential
for Self-discovery.

"

"

Ignorance causes the mistaken
identification of the Self with the
mind's attributes, but discernment
reveals the Self's true,
unchanging nature.

41

ज्ञातृज्ञानज्ञेयभेदः परे नात्मनि विद्यते ।
चिदानन्दैकरूपत्वाद्दीप्यते स्वयमेव तत् ॥

jñātṛ-jñāna-jñeya-bhedaḥ pare nātmai vidyate ।
cidānandaikarūpatvād dīpyate svayam eva tat ॥

ज्ञातृ (jñātṛ): knower; ज्ञान (jñāna): knowledge; ज्ञेय (jñeya): known; भेदः (bhedaḥ): distinction; परे (pare): in the supreme; न (na): not; आत्मनि (Ātmani): in the Self; विद्यते (vidyate): exists; चित् (cit): consciousness; आनन्द (ānanda): bliss; एकरूपत्वात् (ekarūpatvāt): due to the nature of being one; दीप्यते (dīpyate): shines; स्वयम् (svayam): itself; एव (eva): indeed; तत् (tat): that.

> **In the Supreme Self, there is no distinction between the knower, knowledge, and the known. Being of the nature of one consciousness-bliss, it shines by itself.**

This verse explains the non-dual nature of the Self, emphasizing the absence of distinctions within the supreme reality. It highlights that in the ultimate realm of the Self, there are no separations between the knower, knowledge, and the known, as these distinctions are mere constructs of the empirical world. In the Self, dualities dissolve, revealing an underlying unity.

The Self is pure consciousness and bliss, Self-luminous and Self-evident, requiring no external validation. The phrase "shines by itself" underscores the Self's Self-revealing nature, unlike worldly objects that need light to be perceived.

This verse encourages the seeker to transcend the dualities of the world and realize the unity of the Self.

42

एवमात्मारणौ ध्यानमथने सततं कृते ।
उदितावगतिज्वला सर्वाज्ञानेन्धनं दहेत् ॥

evam ātmāraṇau dhyānamathane satataṃ kṛte ।
uditāvagatir jvālā sarvājñānendhanaṃ dahet ॥

एवम् (evam): thus; आत्म (Ātma): Self; अरणौ (araṇau): in the fire stick; ध्यान (dhyāna): meditation; मथने (mathane): churning; सततम् (satatam): continuously; कृते (kṛte): done; उदिता (uditā): arisen; अवगतिः (avagatiḥ): knowledge; ज्वाला (jvālā): flame; सर्व (sarva): all; अज्ञान (ajñāna): ignorance; इन्धनम् (indhanam): fuel; दहेत् (dahet): burns.

> **Meditating on the Self is like rubbing two sticks together. Eventually, the fire of true understanding ignites and burns away all ignorance.**

This verse uses the metaphor of fire sticks to illustrate the process of meditation leading to enlightenment. The intellect is likened to a fire stick, and meditation is the churning that ignites the flame of knowledge. Just as physical fire is produced through persistent churning, spiritual knowledge arises from sustained meditation.

Once kindled, this flame of knowledge burns away ignorance (ajñāna), the root cause of suffering and the illusion of duality. By eliminating ignorance, the practitioner gains clarity and realizes the non-dual nature of reality, recognizing their true nature as the Self, identical with Brahman.

The verse emphasizes the importance of perseverance in meditation and highlights the transformative power of knowledge. This process leads to Self-realization, freeing one from ignorance and revealing the ultimate truth.

~

43

अरुणेनेव बोधेन पूर्वं सन्तमसे हृते ।
तत आविर्भवेदात्मा स्वयमेवांशुमानिव ॥

aruṇeneva bodhena pūrvaṃ santamase hṛte ।
tata āvirbhaved ātmā svayam evāṃśumān iva ॥

अरुणेन (aruṇena): by the dawn; इव (iva): like; बोधेन (bodhena): by knowledge; पूर्वम् (pūrvaṃ): first; सन्तमसे (santamase): darkness; हृते (hṛte): removed; ततः (tataḥ): then; आविर्भवेत् (āvirbhavet): manifests; आत्मा (Ātmā): Self; स्वयम् (svayam): itself; एव (eva): indeed; अंशुमान् (aṃśumān): the Sun.

> **Just as the darkness is dispelled by the dawn (aruna) bringing light, the Self (Ātma) reveals itself, shining forth like the Sun, on its own.**

This verse uses the metaphor of dawn dispelling darkness to illustrate the transformative power of knowledge in revealing the Self. The dawn represents knowledge (bodha), while darkness symbolizes ignorance (avidyā). The process begins with the removal of ignorance, much like the first light of dawn eliminates the night's darkness. This is crucial because ignorance is the root cause of suffering and the perception of duality.

Knowledge in this context is the understanding of one's true nature as the Self (Ātma), non-different from Brahman, the ultimate reality. Once ignorance is dispelled, the Self naturally shines forth, just as the Sun becomes visible after darkness is removed. The Self is inherently Self-luminous and ever-present, but it is obscured by ignorance. When ignorance is removed, the Self reveals itself in its true form—pure consciousness and bliss.

44

आत्मा तु सततं प्राप्तोऽप्यप्राप्तवदविद्यया ।
तन्नाशे प्राप्तवद्भाति स्वकण्ठाभरणं यथा ॥

Ātmā tu satataṃ prāpto'pyaprāptavad avidyayā ।
tannāśe prāptavad bhāti svakaṇṭhābharaṇaṃ yathā ॥

आत्मा (Ātmā): the Self; तु (tu): indeed; सततम् (satataṃ): always; प्राप्तः (prāptaḥ): attained; अपि (api): even though; अप्राप्तवत् (aprāptavat): as if not attained; अविद्यया (avidyayā): due to ignorance; तत् (tat): that; नाशे (nāśe): when destroyed; प्राप्तवत् (prāptavat): as if attained; भाति (bhāti): shines; स्वकण्ठ (svakaṇṭha): own neck; आभरणम् (ābharaṇam): ornament; यथा (yathā): like.

> **The Self is ever-present, but due to ignorance, it seems unattained. When ignorance is dispelled, the Self reveals itself, appearing as though newly discovered—just like finding a necklace around your neck that you thought was lost.**

This verse highlights the paradox of Self-realization. Ignorance creates a veil that obscures the true nature of the Self, making individuals perceive themselves as separate and limited beings. The Self is ever-present and already attained, but appears unattained due to ignorance (avidyā).

The analogy of a necklace around one's neck illustrates this concept. Just as a person might forget they are wearing a necklace and search for it elsewhere, individuals often seek fulfillment outside themselves, unaware that the Self is already complete within.

When ignorance is removed through knowledge and Self-inquiry, the Self is recognized, much like suddenly noticing the necklace that has been there all along. The Self, being Self-luminous and ever-present, becomes clear once ignorance is dispelled.

This verse emphasizes that Self-realization is not about acquiring something new, but recognizing what is inherently present.

~

45

स्थाणौ पुरुषवद्भ्रान्त्या कृता ब्रह्मणि जीवता ।
जीवस्य तात्त्विके रूपे तस्मिन्दृष्टे निवर्तते ॥

sthāṇau puruṣavad bhrāntyā kṛtā brahmaṇi jīvatā ।
jīvasya tāttvike rūpe tasmin dṛṣṭe nivartate ॥

स्थाणौ (sthāṇau): in a post; पुरुषवत् (puruṣavat): like a man; भ्रान्त्या (bhrāntyā): by delusion; कृता (kṛtā): made; ब्रह्मणि (brahmaṇi): in Brahman; जीवता (jīvatā): the notion of ego-Self or individuality; जीवस्य (jīvasya): of the individual soul; तात्त्विके (tāttvike): true; रूपे (rūpe): nature; तस्मिन् (tasmin): in that; दृष्टे (dṛṣṭe): when seen; निवर्तते (nivartate): ceases.

> **Believing we are separate from the ultimate reality (Brahman) is like mistaking a post for a person in the dark. Once we realize our true nature, this illusion dissolves.**

This verse uses the analogy of mistaking a post for a man to explain the concept of superimposition (adhyāsa), where false attributes are projected due to ignorance. Just as poor visibility or fear leads to the post being seen as a man, ignorance (avidyā) causes the notion of individuality to be falsely superimposed on Brahman, the ultimate reality.

This leads to the perception of the Self as limited and separate, which is the root cause of suffering and bondage. When the true nature of the individual soul (jīva) is realized as non-different from Brahman, the misconception ceases, similar to recognizing the post as a post and not a man.

Self-realization involves understanding that the individual Self (Ātma) is not separate from Brahman. This realization dissolves the illusion of separateness. The verse underscores the importance of discerning the true nature of the Self to overcome ignorance.

"

Once ignorance is dispelled, the
Self naturally shines forth, just as
the Sun becomes visible after
darkness is removed.

"

The sense of individual doership
arises from mistakenly identifying the
Self with the intellect. Through
discernment, one can recognize the
Self as pure awareness,
transcending the ego and
achieving true Self-knowledge.

46

तत्त्वस्वरूपानुभवादुत्पन्नं ज्ञानमंजसा ।
अहं ममेति चाज्ञानं बाधते दिग्भ्रमादिवत् ॥

tattvasvarūpānubhāvād utpannaṃ jñānam añjasā ।
ahaṃ mameti cājñānaṃ bādhate digbhramādivat ॥

तत्त्व (tattva): reality; स्वरूप (svarūpa): true nature; अनुभवात् (anubhāvāt): from the experience; उत्पन्नम् (utpannam): arisen; ज्ञानम् (jñānam): knowledge; अंजसा (añjasā): directly; अहम् (ahaṃ): I; मम (mama): mine; इति (iti): thus; च (ca): and; अज्ञानम् (ajñānam): ignorance; बाधते (bādhate): destroys; दिग्भ्रमादिवत् (digbhramādivat): like the misconception of directions.

> **When you directly experience the true nature of Reality, the knowledge that comes from this immediately removes the false ideas of 'I' and 'mine', just like sunrise clears up confusion about which direction is which.**

This verse emphasizes the transformative power of true knowledge in dispelling ignorance and realizing one's true nature. It explains that the experiential understanding of one's identity with Brahman leads to the spontaneous arising of knowledge, not just intellectual but deeply realized.

Ignorance, characterized by the notions of 'I' (aham) and 'mine' (mama), stems from false identification with the body and mind, creating a sense of separateness. The analogy of being lost and finding the correct direction (digbhrama) illustrates how this realization dispels ignorance, just as understanding one's true direction clears confusion.

Once ignorance is removed, the individual recognizes their true nature as non-different from Brahman. The verse underscores the importance of Self-realization in overcoming illusions of ego and attachment, highlighting the profound impact of this knowledge in transforming one's understanding of reality.

47

सम्यग्विज्ञानवान् योगी स्वात्मन्येवाखिलं जगत् ।
एकं च सर्वमात्मानमीक्षते ज्ञानचक्षुषा ॥

samyag-vijñānavān yogī svātma-yevākhilaṃ jagat ।
ekaṃ ca sarvam-ātmānam-īkṣate jñāna-cakṣuṣā ॥

सम्यक् (samyak): properly; विज्ञानवान् (vijñānavān): one who is endowed with wisdom; योगी (yogī): wise person; स्वात्मनि (svātmai): in one's own Self; एव (eva): only; अखिलम् (akhilam): entire; जगत् (jagat): the world; एकम् (ekam): one; च (ca): and; सर्वम् (sarvam): everything; आत्मानम् (Ātmānam): the Ātma; ईक्षते (ikṣate): sees; ज्ञानचक्षुषा (jñāna-cakṣuṣā): with the eyes of knowledge/wisdom.

> **A wise person, through true understanding, perceives the entire world within themselves and recognizes the one Self in all things through the eyes of jñāna (knowledge).**

This verse emphasizes the transformative vision of a yogi or wise person who has attained perfect wisdom. Such a yogi does not see the world as separate from himself. Instead, through deep spiritual insight, he perceives the entire universe as a manifestation within his own Self. This vision of unity is the hallmark of true wisdom, where distinctions between Self and other dissolve, revealing the oneness of all existence.

In the context of spiritual wisdom, this verse points to the ultimate realization that the individual Self and the universal Self are not different. A wise person who reaches this stage of enlightenment sees no separation between himself and the world around him; all distinctions merge into the singular reality of the Self.

This vision is not merely intellectual but is experienced through the "eyes of knowledge," indicating a direct, experiential understanding that transcends ordinary perception. The verse encapsulates the essence of Vedanta, where the Self and the cosmos are understood as one unified reality.

~

48

आत्मैवेदं जगत्सर्वमात्मनोऽन्यन्न विद्यते ।
मृदो यद्वद्घटादीनि स्वात्मानं सर्वमीक्षते ॥

Ātmaivedaṃ jagat-sarvam-ātmao'nyanna vidyate ।
mṛdo yadvat ghaṭādīni svātmānaṃ sarvamīkṣate ॥

आत्मा (Ātmā): the Self; एव (eva): only; इदम् (idam): this; जगत् (jagat): the world; सर्वम् (sarvam): everything; आत्मनः (Ātmaah): of the Self; अन्यत् (anyat): other; न (na): not; विद्यते (vidyate): exists; मृदः (mṛdah): of clay; यद्वत् (yadvat): just as; घटादीनि (ghaṭādīni): pots and other objects; स्वात्मानम् (svātmānam): its own essence, the Self; सर्वम् (sarvam): everything; ईक्षते (ikṣate): sees.

> **Everything in this world is really just the Self; there's nothing that exists apart from the Self. Just as pots and other objects are all made of clay, the wise person sees everything as the Self.**

This verse asserts that the entire universe is nothing but the Self, and there is nothing apart from it, challenging the ordinary perception of distinct entities. Using the analogy of clay and pots, it explains that just as various clay objects are fundamentally clay in different forms, all objects and beings are manifestations of the one Self. Despite the apparent diversity, the underlying reality is the same, just as clay remains the substance of all clay objects.

Recognizing the Self as everything means understanding that all forms, names, and distinctions are expressions of the same fundamental reality. In this state of realization, one perceives no separation between themselves and the world. The verse teaches that the perception of duality is an illusion, and through spiritual wisdom, one realizes that everything is a manifestation of the Self.

Ultimately, this verse invites the seeker to transcend the illusion of multiplicity and realize the non-dual nature of reality, where the Self is the only true existence.

～

49

जीवन्मुक्तस्तु तद्विद्वान्पूर्वोपाधिगुणांस्त्यजेत् ।
सच्चिदानन्दरूपत्वात् भवेद्भ्रमरकीटवत् ॥

jīvanmuktas tu tadvidvān pūrvopādhiguṇāṁs tyaje ।
saccidānandarūpatvāt bhaved bhramarakīṭavat ॥

जीवन्मुक्तः (jīvanmuktaḥ): one who is liberated while living; तु (tu): indeed; तद्विद्वान् (tadvidvān): one who knows that (truth); पूर्व (pūrva): former; उपाधि (upādhi): limitation or conditioning; गुणान् (guṇān): qualities; त्यजेत् (tyajet): should abandon; सत् (sat): existence; चित् (cit): consciousness; आनन्द (ānanda): bliss; रूपत्वात् (rūpatvāt): because of the nature; भवेत् (bhavet): becomes; भ्रमरकीटवत् (bhramarakīṭavat): like the wasp and the wasp-larva.

> **A jīvanmukta (liberated being) is one who has realized the truth and transcends the limitations of the body and mind. Being of the nature of sat-cit-ānanda (existence, consciousness, and bliss), they undergo a complete transformation, like a wasp larva transforming into a wasp.**

This verse describes the state of a jīvanmukta, a person who attains liberation while still living, having realized their identity with Brahman, the absolute reality characterized by existence (sat), consciousness (cit), and bliss (ānanda). The verse emphasizes that the liberated individual should abandon qualities tied to previous limitations or conditionings (upādhis), such as ego and individuality, which arise from ignorance.

The analogy of bhramara-kīṭa-vat (like the wasp and the wasp-larva) illustrates this transformation, similar to how a larva transforms into a wasp. Just as the larva undergoes a complete change, the individual Self, through the realization of its true nature, sees itself as Brahman.

This transformation signifies the shedding of false identifications and the recognition of one's essence as non-different from Brahman. A jīvanmukta lives free from the bondage of ignorance, experiencing the unity of existence, consciousness, and bliss, embodying the ultimate goal of liberation, leading to a life of freedom and fulfillment.

～

50

तीर्त्वा मोहार्णवं हत्वा रागद्वेषादिराक्षसान् ।
योगी शान्तिसमायुक्त आत्मारामो विराजते ॥

tīrtvā mohārṇavaṃ hatvā rāgadveṣādirākṣasān ।
yogī śāntisamāyukta ātmārāmo virājate ॥

तीर्त्वा (tīrtvā): having crossed; मोह (moha): delusion; आर्णवम् (ārṇavam): ocean; हत्वा (hatvā): having slain; राग (rāga): attachment; द्वेष (dveṣa): aversion; आदि (ādi): and others; राक्षसान् (rākṣasān): demons; योगी (yogī): the yogi; शान्ति (śānti): peace; समायुक्त (samāyukta): endowed with; आत्मारामः (Ātmārāmah): rejoicing in the Self; विराजते (virājate): shines.

> **Having crossed the ocean of delusion and slain the demons of dualities (attachments and aversions), the yogi, united with peace, shines forth, rejoicing in the Self.**

This verse metaphorically describes the spiritual journey and the state of a realized yogi, someone who has attained liberation. The "ocean of delusion" (mohārṇava) represents the ignorance that engulfs individuals, leading them to identify with the transient aspects of existence. Crossing this ocean symbolizes overcoming ignorance and the illusions of the material world.

The "demons of attachment and aversion" (raga-dveṣādi -rākṣasān) represent internal obstacles such as desires and negative emotions. Slaying these demons signifies mastering emotions and achieving detachment from worldly entanglements.

The yogi, now endowed with profound inner peace, finds fulfillment within, independent of external circumstances, "rejoicing in the Self" (Ātmārāmaḥ). The yogi "shines," radiating clarity and alignment with their true nature, reflecting the realization of the Self as non-different from Brahman, the ultimate reality.

～

"

The Self (Ātma) is pure, unchanging consciousness, while the intellect is merely reflecting the Self's light. Due to ignorance, the individual soul (jīva) mistakenly identifies with the intellect's functions. But through discernment, one can realize the Self as the eternal witness, beyond the intellect and its activities.

"

Fear and suffering arise from the
mistaken identification of the Self
with the ego-self. Only through
discernment and Self-knowledge,
one realizes the Self as the eternal
unchanging Reality, leading to
freedom from fear.

51

बाह्यानित्यसुखासक्तिं हित्वात्मसुखनिर्वृतः ।
घटस्थदीपवत्स्वस्थः स्वान्तरेव प्रकाशते ॥

bāhyānityasukhāsaktiṃ hitvātmāsukhanirvṛtaḥ ।
ghaṭasthadīpavat svasthaḥ svāntareva prakāśate ॥

बाह्य (bāhya): external; अनित्य (anitya): impermanent; सुखासक्तिम् (sukhāsaktiṃ): attachment to pleasure; हित्वा (hitvā): having abandoned; आत्म (Ātma): Self; सुख (sukha): bliss; निर्वृतः (nirvṛtaḥ): contented; घटस्थ-दीपवत् (ghaṭastha-dīpavat): like a lamp inside a pot; स्वस्थः (svasthaḥ): abiding in oneself; स्वान्तरे (svāntare): within oneself; एव (eva): indeed; प्रकाशते (prakāśate): shines.

> **Letting go of attachment to fleeting external pleasures and finding joy in the Self, the wise one shines from within, like a lamp inside a pot.**

This verse emphasizes the inner journey of Self-realization and the contentment that arises from it. It begins by stressing the need to renounce attachment to external, transient pleasures, as they lead to cycles of desire and dissatisfaction. True contentment is found in the bliss of the Self (Ātmāsukha), which is constant and independent of external circumstances, bringing profound fulfillment and peace.

The analogy of a lamp inside a pot (ghaṭastha-dīpavat) illustrates the Self-luminous nature of a realized individual. Like a lamp shining within, the realized soul radiates Self-awareness and peace from within, unaffected by external conditions.

The verse concludes by affirming that this inner radiance results from abiding in oneself, leading to a stable, Self-sufficient state of peace and contentment. Free from external disturbances, the realized person experiences unwavering tranquility and fulfillment.

52

उपाधिस्थोऽपि तद्धर्मैरलिप्तो व्योमवन्मुनिः ।
सर्वविन्मूढवत्तिष्ठेदसक्तो वायुवच्चरेत् ॥

upādhistho'pi taddharmair alipto vyomavan muniḥ ।
sarvavit mūḍhavat tiṣṭhed asakto vāyuvat caret ॥

उपाधिस्थः अपि (upādhisthaḥ api): even though situated in conditionings; तत् (tat): their; धर्मैः (dharmaiḥ): by the qualities; अलिप्तः (aliptaḥ): unattached; व्योमवत् (vyomavat): like space; मुनिः (muniḥ): the sage; सर्ववित् (sarvavit): knower of all; मूढवत् (mūḍhavat): like a fool; तिष्ठेत् (tiṣṭhet): should remain; असक्तः (asaktaḥ): unattached; वायुवत् (vāyuvat): like the wind; चरेत् (caret): should move.

> **Even though the liberated person is situated in limitations and conditionings, he remains unattached to their qualities, like space. The sage, who is the knower of all appears, like a fool and moves like the wind, unattached.**

This verse describes the state of a realized sage who has attained Self-realization and lives in the world without being affected by it. Though the sage exists within the limitations of the body and mind, they remain unattached to these conditionings, much like space remains unaffected by the objects within it. This detachment allows the sage to maintain inner peace and equanimity.

The sage is a knower of all, possessing deep wisdom and understanding of the oneness of all existence. To the unknowing, the sage may appear foolish because they do not conform to societal norms or display typical worldly wisdom, reflecting their detachment from ego and worldly concerns.

Moving through life with freedom and non-attachment, like the wind, the sage interacts with the world without becoming entangled in it. The verse highlights the qualities of detachment, wisdom, and freedom, showing how a realized sage can live fully engaged in the world yet remain unaffected by its limitations, embodying liberation and inner peace.

~

उपाधिविलयाद्विष्णौ निर्विशेषं विशेन्मुनिः ।
जले जलं वियद्व्योम्नि तेजस्तेजसि वा यथा ॥

upādhivilayād viṣṇau nirviśeṣaṃ viśen muniḥ ।
jale jalaṃ viyad vyomni tejas tejasi vā yathā ॥

उपाधि (upādhi): limitation or conditioning; विलयात् (vilayāt): from dissolution; विष्णौ (viṣṇau): in Vishnu (the all-pervading reality); निर्विशेषम् (nirviśeṣam): without distinction; विशेत् (viśet): enters; मुनिः (muniḥ): the sage; जले (jale): in water; जलम् (jalam): water; वियत् (viyat): space; व्योम्नि (vyomni): in space; तेजः (tejaḥ): light; तेजसि (tejasi): in light; वा (vā): or; यथा (yathā): like.

> **When the conditionings are dissolved, the liberated sage becomes one with Vishnu, the all-pervading reality, just as water dissolves into water, space into space, or light into light.**

This verse describes the ultimate realization and merging of the individual Self with the supreme reality, represented here by Vishnu, the all-pervading and infinite consciousness. The process of dissolution of limitations (upādhis) refers to the shedding of all individual conditionings and identifications, such as the ego, body, and mind, which create a sense of separateness.

The sage, upon realizing their true nature, merges into the undifferentiated reality of Brahman, just as water merges seamlessly into water, space into space, and light into light. These analogies illustrate the idea of complete unity and non-distinction, where the individual Self is no longer perceived as separate from the universal Self.

This merging signifies the state of liberation (mokṣa), where the sage transcends all dualities and distinctions, experiencing the oneness of existence. The verse emphasizes the natural and effortless nature of this realization, as it is akin to elements merging with their own kind, highlighting the intrinsic unity of all existence.

यल्लाभान्नापरो लाभो यत्सुखान्नापरं सुखम् ।
यज्ज्ञानान्नापरं ज्ञानं तद्ब्रह्मेत्यवधारयेत् ॥

yallābhān nāparo lābho yatsukhān nāparaṃ sukham ।
yajjñānān nāparaṃ jñānaṃ tad brahmety avadhārayet ॥

यत् लाभात् (yat lābhāt): by gaining which; न (na): not; अपरः (aparaḥ): another; लाभः (lābhaḥ): gain; यत् (yat): by which; सुखात् (sukhāt): happiness; न (na): not; अपरम् (aparam): another; सुखम् (sukham): happiness; यत् (yat): by which; ज्ञानात् (jñānāt): knowledge; न (na): not; अपरम् (aparam): another; ज्ञानम् (jñānam): knowledge; तत् (tat): that; ब्रह्म (brahma): Brahman; इति (iti): thus; अवधारयेत् (avadhārayet): should understand or realize.

> **Understand that Brahman is that which, once attained, leaves nothing more to gain; once experienced, no greater joy exists; and once known, there's nothing left to know.**

This verse emphasizes the supreme and unparalleled nature of the ultimate reality. Brahman is described as the ultimate gain, such that once it is attained, there is nothing else to be sought, fulfilling all desires and aspirations.

The happiness derived from realizing Brahman is infinite and eternal, transcending worldly pleasures that are temporary and limited. Additionally, the knowledge of Brahman is the highest form of understanding, revealing the true nature of reality and the Self, surpassing all intellectual or empirical knowledge.

The verse encourages seekers to pursue Brahman as the ultimate goal of life, encompassing the highest gain, happiness, and knowledge. By internalizing this truth, one can transcend dualities and experience the oneness of all existence.

～

यद्दृष्ट्वा नापरं दृश्यं यद्भूत्वा न पुनर्भवः ।
यज्ज्ञात्वा नापरं ज्ञेयं तद्ब्रह्मेत्यवधारयेत् ॥

yad dṛṣṭvā nāparaṃ dṛśyaṃ yad bhūtvā na punar bhavaḥ ।
yajjñātvā nāparaṃ jñeyaṃ tad brahmety avadhārayet ॥

यत् (yat): that which; दृष्ट्वा (dṛṣṭvā): having seen; न (na): not; अपरम् (aparam): another; दृश्यम् (dṛśyam): object to be seen; यत् (yat): that which; भूत्वा (bhūtvā): having become; न (na): not; पुनः (punaḥ): again; भवः (bhavaḥ): birth; यत् (yat): that which; ज्ञात्वा (jñātvā): having known; न (na): not; अपरम् (aparam): another; ज्ञेयम् (jñeyam): thing to be known; तत् (tat): that; ब्रह्म (brahma): Brahman; इति (iti): thus; अवधारयेत् (avadhārayet): should understand or realize.

> **Understand that Brahman is that which, once seen, leaves nothing else to be seen; once become, frees you from rebirth; and once known, leaves nothing else to know.**

This verse highlights the ultimate realization and fulfillment found in Brahman, focusing on three key aspects. First, it states that once Brahman is realized, there is nothing else to be seen, as it encompasses the truth beyond all appearances and forms.

Second, it mentions that becoming one with Brahman leads to liberation (mokṣa), freeing the jīva from the cycle of samsara and transcending the limitations of the material world. Third, knowing Brahman means nothing else remains to be known, as this knowledge is complete and reveals the essence of all existence.

The verse encourages seekers to prioritize the realization of Brahman as the ultimate goal, leading to the end of dualities and the fulfillment of spiritual enlightenment. It emphasizes that this realization brings true completeness and liberation.

∼

"

Knowledge is compared to dawn dispelling darkness, as it removes ignorance and reveals the true nature of the Self.

"

Self-realization is the recognition
that the ever-present Self is
obscured by ignorance, leading to
the false perception of separation.
Once ignorance is dispelled, the true
nature of the Self is revealed.

56

तिर्यगूर्ध्वमधः पूर्णं सच्चिदानन्दमद्वयम् ।
अनन्तं नित्यमेकं यत्तद्ब्रह्मेत्यवधारयेत् ॥

tiryagūrdhvamadhaḥ pūrṇaṃ saccidānandamadvayam |
anantaṃ nityam ekaṃ yat tad brahmety avadhārayet ||

तिर्यक् (tiryak): horizontal; ऊर्ध्वम् (ūrdhvam): above; अधः (adhaḥ): below; पूर्णम् (pūrṇam): full; सत् (sat): existence; चित् (cit): consciousness; आनन्दम् (ānandam): bliss; अद्वयम् (advayam): non-dual; अनन्तम् (anantam): infinite; नित्यम् (nityam): eternal; एकम् (ekam): one; यत् (yat): that which; तत् (tat): that; ब्रह्म (brahma): Brahman; इति (iti): thus; अवधारयेत् (avadhārayet): should understand.

> **Understand that Brahman is that which is complete in every direction - up, down, and all around. It is sat, cit, and ānanda. It is without a second, endless, always existing, and one.**

This verse describes Brahman, the ultimate reality, as all-encompassing, non-dual, and ever-present. Brahman is full (pūrṇa) in all directions—horizontally, above, and below—indicating its omnipresence and omnipotence.

Characterized by sat (existence), cit (consciousness), and ānanda (bliss), Brahman is the source of all being, the consciousness that illuminates experience, and the essence of true happiness. The terms advayam (non-dual), anantam (infinite), and nityam (eternal) highlight Brahman's unity, limitlessness, and time-lessness.

The verse encourages seekers to realize Brahman's comprehensive nature, transcending all limitations and distinctions. This realization leads to liberation, freeing one from the illusions of duality and separate-ness, and is the essence of spiritual enlightenment.

~

57

अतद्व्यावृत्तिरूपेण वेदान्तैर्लक्ष्यतेऽद्वयम् ।
अखण्डानन्दमेकं यत्तद्ब्रह्मेत्यवधारयेत् ॥

atadvyāvṛttirūpeṇa vedāntair lakṣyate'dvayam ।
akhaṇḍānandam ekaṃ yat tad brahmety avadhārayet ॥

अतद्व्यावृत्ति (atad-vyāvṛtti): by negating what is not; रूपेण (rūpeṇa): in the form; वेदान्तैः (vedāntaiḥ): by the vedanta; लक्ष्यते (lakṣyate): is indicated; अद्वयम् (advayam): non-dual; अखण्डानन्दम् (akhaṇḍānandam): indivisible bliss; एकम् (ekam): one; यत् (yat): that which; तत् (tat): that; ब्रह्म (brahma): Brahman; इति (iti): thus; अवधारयेत् (avadhārayet): should understand or realize.

> **Understand that Brahman is what the Vedanta point to by saying 'not this, not this'. It is without a second, unbroken joy, and completely one.**

This verse describes the method by which Vedanta indicates the nature of Brahman. It uses the process of "neti neti" (not this, not this) to negate all that is not Brahman, thereby pointing to what Brahman truly is. This method helps in understanding Brahman as the ultimate reality that is beyond all attributes and dualities.

Brahman is described as "advayam," meaning non-dual, emphasizing its nature as the singular reality without a second. It is also characterized by "akhaṇḍānandam," which means indivisible bliss, highlighting that Brahman is the source of ultimate and unbroken happiness.

The term "ekam" underscores the oneness of Brahman, reinforcing the idea that it is the singular, unified essence of all that exists. This understanding is central to Vedanta, which asserts that the apparent multiplicity of the world is an illusion, and only Brahman is real.

The verse encourages seekers to realize this truth through the teachings of Vedanta, leading to the ultimate realization of Brahman and the experience of liberation (mokṣa).

58

अखण्डानन्दरूपस्य तस्यानन्दलवाश्रिताः ।
ब्रह्माद्यास्तारतम्येन भवन्त्यानन्दिनोऽखिलाः ॥

akhaṇḍānandarūpasya tasyānandalavāśritāḥ ।
brahmādyās tāratamyena bhavanty ānandino'khilāḥ ॥

अखण्डानन्दरूपस्य (akhaṇḍānandarūpasya): of the nature of indivisible bliss; तस्य (tasya): of that; आनन्दलवाश्रिताः (ānandalavāśritāḥ): dependent on a fraction of bliss; ब्रह्माद्याः (brahmādyāḥ): brahma and others; तारतम्येन (tāratamyena): in gradation; भवन्ति (bhavanti): become; आनन्दिनः (ānandinaḥ): blissful; अखिलाः (akhilāḥ): all.

> **All creatures, from the highest God Brahma to the lowest, experience happiness to different degrees. But this happiness is just a tiny part of the complete, unbroken bliss that is Brahman.**

This verse illustrates the infinite and indivisible nature of bliss that is intrinsic to Brahman, the ultimate reality. It explains that Brahman embodies a state of unbroken and limitless joy, from which all other beings derive their own experiences of happiness.

While higher beings may experience greater levels of bliss, it remains a mere reflection of Brahman's unbounded joy. This teaching highlights the limitations of worldly and divine pleasures when compared to the infinite essence of Brahman.

The verse encourages seekers to move beyond temporary and limited experiences toward the realization of Brahman, where they can access the true, unending, and indivisible bliss that transcends all distinctions.

∼

59

तद्युक्तमखिलं वस्तु व्यवहारस्तदन्वितः ।
तस्मात्सर्वगतं ब्रह्म क्षीरे सर्पिरिवाखिले ॥

tadyuktam akhilaṃ vastu vyavahāras tad-anvitaḥ ।
tasmāt sarvagataṃ brahma kṣīre sarpir ivākhile ॥

तत् (tat): that; युक्तम् (yuktam): united; अखिलम् (akhilam): entire; वस्तु (vastu): object; व्यवहारः (vyavahārah): activity; तत् (tat): that; अन्वितः (anvitaḥ): endowed with; तस्मात् (tasmāt): therefore; सर्वगतम् (sarvagatam): all-pervading; ब्रह्म (brahma): Brahman; क्षीरे (kṣīre): in milk; सर्पिः (sarpiḥ): butter; इव (iva): like; अखिले (akhile): in all.

> **Everything is filled with Brahman, and all activities happen because of It. So Brahman is everywhere, just like butter is present throughout milk.**

This verse emphasizes the omnipresence and integral nature of Brahman in all aspects of existence. It suggests that every object and activity in the universe is connected to and supported by Brahman. This connection implies that nothing exists independently of Brahman, highlighting its role as the fundamental reality underlying all phenomena.

The analogy of butter in milk illustrates this concept. Just as butter is present throughout milk, even though it is not immediately visible, Brahman pervades all creation, though it may not be directly perceived. The process of churning milk to reveal butter is akin to spiritual practices that lead to the realization of Brahman's presence.

The verse concludes by affirming that Brahman is all-pervading, meaning it exists everywhere and in everything. This understanding encourages the seeker to recognize the divine presence in all aspects of life and to realize the unity of existence. Such realization leads to a deeper appreciation of the interconnectedness of all things and the ultimate reality that is Brahman.

60

अनण्वस्थूलमह्रस्वमदीर्घमजमव्ययम् ।
अरूपगुणवर्णाख्यं तद्ब्रह्मेत्यवधारयेत् ॥

anaṇvasthūlam ahrasvam adīrgham ajam avyayam ।
arūpaguṇavarṇākhyaṃ tad brahmety avadhārayet ॥

अनणु (anaṇu): not minute; अस्थूलम् (asthūlam): not large; अह्रस्वम् (ahrasvam): not short; अदीर्घम् (adīrgham): not long; अजम् (ajam): unborn; अव्ययम् (avyayam): imperishable; अरूप (arūpa): formless; अगुण (aguṇa): attributeless; अवर्ण (avarṇa): colorless; आख्यम् (ākhyam): nameless; तत् (tat): that; ब्रह्म (brahma): Brahman; इति (iti): thus; अवधारयेत् (avadhārayet): should understand.

One should understand that Brahman is that which is neither minute nor large, neither short nor long. It is unborn, imperishable. It is formless, attributeless, colorless, and nameless.

This verse describes the nature of Brahman by negating any physical attributes or limitations, emphasizing that Brahman transcends all dimensions and measurements. It is described as unborn and imperishable, highlighting its eternal and unchanging nature, unlike entities in the material world that undergo birth, change, and decay.

Brahman is formless, attributeless, colorless, and nameless, existing beyond all descriptions and conceptualizations. This reinforces that Brahman cannot be confined to any specific form, quality, or identity.

The verse encourages seekers to transcend the limitations of perception and thought to realize Brahman as the ultimate reality, beyond all forms and attributes.

~

"

Superimposition (adhyāsa) causes the illusion of individuality, where the Self is mistakenly seen as separate from Brahman due to ignorance. Realizing the Self's true nature dissolves this illusion.

"

A wise yogi sees the entire universe
as a manifestation within his own
Self, perceiving no separation
between himself and the world.
This realization of oneness through
direct experience is the essence
of true wisdom.

61

यद्भासा भास्यतेऽर्कादि भास्यैर्यत्तु न भास्यते ।
येन सर्वमिदं भाति तद्ब्रह्मेत्यवधारयेत् ॥

yad bhāsā bhāsyate'rkādi bhāsyair yat tu na bhāsyate ।
yena sarvam idaṃ bhāti tad brahmety avadhārayet ॥

यत् (yat): that which; भासा (bhāsā): by the light; भास्यते (bhāsyate): is illuminated; अर्कादि (arkādi): the Sun and others; भास्यैः (bhāsyaiḥ): by those which are illuminated; यत् (yat): that which; तु (tu): but; न (na): not; भास्यते (bhāsyate): is illuminated; येन (yena): by which; सर्वम् (sarvam): all; इदम् (idam): this; भाति (bhāti): shines; तत् (tat): that; ब्रह्म (brahma): Brahman; इति (iti): thus; अवधारयेत् (avadhārayet): should understand.

> **Understand that Brahman is that which gives light to the Sun and others, but isn't illuminated by them. It's that by which everything shines.**

This verse highlights the concept of Brahman as the ultimate source of all illumination and existence. It emphasizes that Brahman is the fundamental reality that illuminates everything, including the Sun and other sources of light. However, Brahman itself is Self-luminous and does not require any external source for its illumination.

The phrase "by which all this shines" indicates that Brahman is the underlying reality that enables the manifestation and perception of the universe. Everything that exists derives its ability to shine or be perceived from Brahman.

This understanding encourages seekers to recognize Brahman as the ultimate truth and source of all existence. By realizing this, one transcends the limitations of the material world and perceives the unity and oneness of all that exists.

62

स्वयमन्तर्बहिर्व्याप्य भासयन्नखिलं जगत् ।
ब्रह्म प्रकाशते वह्निप्रतप्तायसपिण्डवत् ॥

svayam antarbahir vyāpya bhāsayann akhilaṃ jagat ।
brahma prakāśate vahniprataptāyasapiṇḍavat ॥

स्वयम् (svayam): itself; अन्तः (antaḥ): within; बहि: (bahiḥ): outside; व्याप्य (vyāpya): pervading; भासयन् (bhāsayan): illuminating; अखिलम् (akhilam): entire; जगत् (jagat): world; ब्रह्म (brahma): Brahman; प्रकाशते (prakāśate): shines; वह्नि-प्रतप्त-आयस-पिण्डवत् (vahni-prataptāyasa-piṇḍavat): like a piece of iron heated by fire.

> **Brahman spreads through everything, inside and out, lighting up the whole world. It shines like an iron ball that's been heated red-hot in fire.**

This verse describes the omnipresence and illuminating nature of Brahman, the ultimate reality. Brahman is said to pervade both within and outside, signifying its all-encompassing presence in every aspect of existence. This indicates that Brahman is not confined to any particular location or entity but is the underlying reality of everything.

The analogy of a piece of iron heated by fire illustrates how Brahman imparts its light and consciousness to the world. Just as a piece of iron glows when heated by fire, the world shines with the light of Brahman. This highlights the idea that all illumination and consciousness in the universe are manifestations of Brahman's inherent nature.

By understanding Brahman as the source of all light and consciousness, one can recognize the unity and interconnectedness of all things.

63

जगद्विलक्षणं ब्रह्म ब्रह्मणोऽन्यन्न किंचन ।
ब्रह्मान्यद्भाति चेन्मिथ्या यथा मरुमरीचिका ॥

jagadvilakṣaṇaṃ brahma brahmaṇo'nyan na kiñcana ।
brahmānyad bhāti cen mithyā yathā marumarīcikā ॥

जगत् (jagat): the world; विलक्षणम् (vilakṣaṇam): distinct; ब्रह्म (brahma): Brahman; ब्रह्मणः (brahmaṇaḥ): from Brahman; अन्यत् (anyat): other; न (na): not; किञ्चन (kiñcana): anything; ब्रह्म (brahma): Brahman; अन्यत् (anyat): other; भाति (bhāti): appears; चेत् (cet): if; मिथ्या (mithyā): illusory; यथा (yathā): like; मरु-मरीचिका (maru-marīcikā): mirage in the desert.

> **Brahman is distinct from the world we see. Nothing exists except Brahman. If anything else seems to exist, it's not real - just like a mirage in the desert.**

This verse describes that Brahman is fundamentally distinct from the world, meaning that the ultimate reality is different from the transient and illusory nature of the material world.

The verse further states that there is nothing other than Brahman. This highlights the idea that Brahman is the sole reality, and everything else that appears to exist is merely an illusion or a misperception, much like a mirage in the desert. A mirage appears real from a distance but vanishes upon closer inspection, revealing its illusory nature.

From the perspective of ignorance, the world is illusory (mithyā) and distinct from Brahman. But from the perspective of knowledge, the world is understood as Brahman itself (satyam).

∽

64

दृश्यते श्रूयते यद्यद्ब्रह्मणोऽन्यन्न तद्भवेत् ।
तत्त्वज्ञानाच्च तद्ब्रह्म सच्चिदानन्दमद्वयम् ॥

dṛśyate śrūyate yadyad brahmaṇo'nyan na tad bhavet ।
tattvajñānāc ca tad brahma saccidānandam advayam ॥

दृश्यते (dṛśyate): is seen; श्रूयते (śrūyate): is heard; यत् यत् (yad yad): whatever; ब्रह्मणः (brahmaṇaḥ): from Brahman; अन्यत् (anyat): other; न (na): not; तत् (tat): that; भवेत् (bhavet): becomes; तत्त्वज्ञानात् (tattvajñānāt): from the knowledge of the truth; च (ca): and; तत् (tat): that; ब्रह्म (brahma): Brahman; सत् (sat): existence; चित् (cit): consciousness; आनन्दम् (ānandam): bliss; अद्वयम् (advayam): non-dual.

> **Whatever you see or hear is nothing other than Brahman. When truth is known, Brahman is realized as existence-consciousness-bliss and non-dual.**

This verse emphasizes the non-dual nature of Brahman and the illusory nature of the world as perceived through the senses. It asserts that anything perceived as separate from Brahman, whether seen or heard, does not truly exist.

The verse further explains that through the knowledge of the truth (tattva-jñāna), one realizes that Brahman is characterized by sat (existence), cit (consciousness), and ānanda (bliss). These attributes describe the essential nature of Brahman as the fundamental reality that is eternal, Self-aware, and inherently blissful.

The term "advayam" highlights the non-dual nature of Brahman, indicating that it is without a second and beyond all dualities. This realization leads to spiritual awakening, where the seeker transcends the illusions of separateness and perceives the unity and oneness of all existence.

65

सर्वगं सच्चिदात्मानं ज्ञानचक्षुर्निरीक्षते ।
अज्ञानचक्षुर्नेक्षेत भास्वन्तं भानुमन्धवत् ॥

sarvagaṃ saccidātmānaṃ jñānacakṣur nirīkṣate ।
ajñānacakṣur naīkṣeta bhāsvantaṃ bhānum andhavat ॥

सर्वगम् (sarvagam): all-pervading; सच्चिदात्मानम् (saccidāt-mānam): the essence of existence and consciousness; ज्ञानचक्षुः (jñānacakṣuḥ): the eye of knowledge; निरीक्षते (nirīkṣate): sees; अज्ञानचक्षुः (ajñānacakṣuḥ): the eye of ignorance; न (na): not; ईक्षेत (ikṣeta): sees; भास्वन्तम् (bhāsvantam): shining; भानुम् (bhānum): the Sun; अन्धवत् (andhavat): like a blind person.

> **The eye of knowledge sees the Self that is everywhere and is pure existence and awareness. But the eye of ignorance can't see it, just like a blind person can't see the bright Sun.**

This verse emphasizes the distinction between true knowledge and ignorance in perceiving Brahman, the all-pervading ultimate reality. Brahman is described as "sarvagam" (all-pervading) and "saccidātmānam" (existence and consciousness), highlighting its omnipresence and role as the essence of all existence.

The "eye of knowledge" (jñānacakṣuḥ) symbolizes the inner vision attained through spiritual insight, allowing one to perceive Brahman, while the "eye of ignorance" (ajñānacakṣuḥ) represents the lack of true understanding, preventing this perception. The verse compares ignorance to blindness, where the Sun shines brightly, but the blind cannot see it, emphasizing how ignorance obscures the perception of reality.

The verse encourages seekers to cultivate true knowledge and wisdom to transcend ignorance and perceive Brahman. By doing so, one realizes the non-dual nature of existence.

"

A Jīvanmukta is someone who attains liberation while alive, realizing their identity with Brahman and shedding false identifications like ego and individuality. This transformation leads to a life of freedom, experiencing the unity of existence, consciousness, and bliss.

"

The realized yogi overcomes
ignorance and inner obstacles,
achieving detachment from worldly
attachments. They find inner peace
and joy within, radiating clarity
through Self-realization and
alignment with their true nature.

66

श्रवणादिभिरुद्दीप्तज्ञानाग्निपरितापितः ।
जीवः सर्वमलान्मुक्तः स्वर्णवद्द्योतते स्वयम् ॥

śravaṇādibhir uddīpta-jñānāgni-paritāpitaḥ ।
jīvaḥ sarva-malān muktaḥ svarṇavad dyotate svayam ॥

श्रवणादिभिः (śravaṇādibhiḥ): through hearing and other practices; उद्दीप्त (uddīpta): ignited; ज्ञानाग्नि (jñānāgni): fire of knowledge; परितापितः (paritāpitaḥ): burned; जीवः (jīvaḥ): the individual soul; सर्वमलान् (sarva-malān): all impurities; मुक्तः (muktaḥ): freed; स्वर्णवत् (svarṇavat): like gold; द्योतते (dyotate): shines; स्वयम् (svayam): by itself.

> **Through hearing and other spiritual practices, the fire of knowledge is ignited, burning away all impurities of the individual soul, which then shines by itself like gold.**

This verse describes the transformative process of spiritual practice, leading to Self-realization. Practices like hearing (śravaṇa), reflection (manana), and meditation (nididhyāsana) ignite the "fire of knowledge" (jñāna-āgni), which burns away all impurities such as ignorance, desires, and attachments.

Once purified, the soul shines by itself, like purified gold revealing its natural brilliance. Just as gold becomes radiant when freed from impurities, the soul reveals its true nature as pure consciousness and bliss when liberated from the obscurations of ignorance.

The verse emphasizes the importance of knowledge and spiritual practice for attaining liberation (mokṣa), highlighting the potential for profound transformation. Through dedicated effort and wisdom, one realizes their true nature, experiencing the Self as radiant, pure, and free.

~

67

हृदाकाशोदितो ह्यात्मा बोधभानुस्तमोऽपहृत् ।
सर्वव्यापी सर्वधारी भाति भासयतेऽखिलम् ॥

hṛdākāśodito hy ātmā bodhabhānus tamo'pahṛt ।
sarvavyāpī sarvadhārī bhāti bhāsayate'khilam ॥

हृदाकाशोदितः (hṛdākāśoditaḥ): arising in the space of the heart; हि (hi): indeed; आत्मा (Ātmā): Self; बोधभानुः (bodhabhānuḥ): Sun of knowledge; तमः (tamaḥ): darkness; अपहृत् (apahṛt): dispelling; सर्वव्यापी (sarvavyāpī): all-pervading; सर्वधारी (sarvadhārī): sustainer of all; भाति (bhāti): shines; भासयते (bhāsayate): illuminates; अखिलम् (akhilam): all.

> **The Self, arising in the space of the heart, is indeed the Sun of knowledge that dispels darkness. It is all-pervading, the sustainer of all, shines, and illuminates everything.**

This verse describes the nature of the Self (Ātmā) as the ultimate source of knowledge and illumination. The Self is said to arise in the "space of the heart" (hṛdākāśa), symbolizing the inner spiritual center where one realizes their true nature. This realization is akin to the "Sun of knowledge" (bodhabhānu), which dispels the "darkness" (tamaḥ) of ignorance and delusion.

The Self is described as "all-pervading" (sarvavyāpī) and the "sustainer of all" (sarvadhārī), emphasizing its omnipresence and fundamental role in supporting the existence of everything. Just as the Sun illuminates the world, the Self shines and illuminates all, revealing the true nature of reality.

This verse encourages seekers to turn inward and realize the Self as the source of all knowledge and light. By dispelling ignorance, one can perceive the unity and interconnectedness of all things, leading to spiritual enlightenment.

~

68

दिग्देशकालाद्यनपेक्ष्य सर्वगं
शीतादिहृन्नित्यसुखं निरंजनम् ।
यः स्वात्मतीर्थं भजते विनिष्क्रियः
स सर्ववित्सर्वगतोऽमृतो भवेत् ॥

digdeśakālādyanapekṣya sarvagaṁ
śītādihṛn nityasukhaṁ nirañjanam ।
yaḥ svātmatīrthaṁ bhajate viniṣkriyaḥ ।
sa sarvavit sarvagato'mṛto bhavet ॥

दिक् (dik): direction; देश (deśa): place; काल (kāla): time; आदि (ādi): etcetera; अनपेक्ष्य (anapekṣya): without dependence; सर्वगम् (sarvagam): all-pervading; शीत (śīta): cold; आदि (ādi): etcetera; हृत् (hṛt): heart; नित्यसुखम् (nityasukham): eternal happiness; निरञ्जनम् (nirañjanam): pure; यः (yaḥ): who; स्वात्म (svātma): own Self; तीर्थम् (tīrtham): sacred space; भजते (bhajate): worships; विनिष्क्रियः (viniṣkriyaḥ): free from action; सः (saḥ): he; सर्ववित् (sarvavit): knower of all; सर्वगतः (sarvagataḥ): all-pervading; अमृतः (amṛtaḥ): immortal; भवेत् (bhavet): becomes.

One who realizes their own Self as the
sacred source, independent of direction,

> **space, time, or external conditions,
> experiences the bliss that is pure, unaffected
> by heat, cold, or dualities. Such a person
> becomes all-knowing, all-encompassing,
> and attains immortality.**

This concluding verse of the Atma Bodha encapsulates the essence of Self-realization and the nature of the Self. It emphasizes that the Self transcends physical limitations like direction, place, time, and other worldly conditions, being all-pervading (sarvagaṁ) and unaffected by external factors such as heat and cold. The Self remains eternally blissful (nitya sukhaṁ) and pure (nirañjanam), free from blemish or dualities.

The verse encourages contemplation (bhajate) of the Self, referred to as svātma-tīrthaṁ—the sacred space within oneself—without needing external rituals or actions (viniṣkriyaḥ). Through this internal journey of Self-awareness, one becomes sarvavit (all-knowing), sarvagataḥ (all-pervading), and amṛtaḥ (immortal), achieving liberation beyond the cycle of birth and death.

The verse underscores that ultimate truth and bliss are found within, independent of external factors, and true liberation comes through Self-contemplation and realization of the Self's eternal presence and knowledge.

॥ इति शंकराचार्यविरचित आत्मबोधः समाप्तः ॥

Iti śaṁkarācārya-viracita Ātmabodhaḥ samāptaḥ ॥

Thus concludes the *Ātma Bodha,* composed by
Ādi Śaṅkarācārya

"

Brahman is non-dual, and
anything perceived as separate
from it is an illusion.

"

The Self is all-pervading, beyond limitations and dualities, remaining eternally blissful and pure. True liberation comes through inward contemplation, realizing the Self as the source of eternal knowledge and immortality.

Resources

For readers interested in exploring *Ātma Bodha* and Advaita Vedanta further, the following resources offer valuable insights:

- **Self-Knowledge (Atmabodha) by Swami Chinmayananda:** A clear and accessible translation with practical commentary, perfect for integrating Vedanta into daily life.

- **Self-Knowledge:** Atmabodha by Swami Nikhilananda: A detailed and scholarly interpretation, offering profound insights into the text.

The following list includes some of the most important texts on Advaita Vedanta, each offering unique insights into the philosophy of non-duality.

These texts, ranging from the profound commentaries on the Upanishads and Bhagavad Gita to the systematic treatises like the Brahma Sutras and Vivekachudamani, provide both theoretical frameworks and practical guidance for the seeker. They explore the nature of the Self, the illusory nature of the world, and the path to realizing one's true identity as non-different from Brahman.

- ❧ **"Bhagavad Gita" with Commentary by Ādi Śaṅkarācārya:** A foundational scripture of Hinduism, with commentary that provides an Advaita Vedanta perspective on the teachings of the Gita. Numerous translations are available online.

- ❧ **"Upanishads" with Commentaries by Ādi Śaṅkarācārya:** Core texts of Vedanta philosophy, with Śaṅkarācārya's commentaries offering insights into the non-dual nature of reality.

- ❧ **"Brahma Sutras" with Commentary by Ādi Śaṅkarācārya:** A critical work that systematically presents the teachings of Vedanta, with Śaṅkarācārya's commentary providing an authoritative interpretation.

- ❧ **"Vivekachudamani" by Ādi Śaṅkarācārya:** A seminal text that offers a detailed guide to the path of self-realization and the principles of non-dualism.

- **"Mandukya Karika" by Gaudapada:** A commentary on the Mandukya Upanishad that elaborates on the concept of non-dualism and the nature of the Self.

- **"Aparokshanubhuti" by Ādi Śaṅkarācārya:** A text that discusses the direct experience of the Self, emphasizing the immediate realization of non-duality.

- **"Panchadasi" by Swami Vidyaranya:** A comprehensive text on Advaita Vedanta that explores the philosophy in detail through fifteen chapters covering different aspects of reality and the Self.

These works are essential reading for anyone serious about understanding Advaita Vedanta.

About the Translator

Dr. Rajeev Kurapati is a physician, philosopher, and writer whose work spans medicine, philosophy, and the study of consciousness. With a deep-rooted passion for both scientific inquiry and ancient wisdom, he explores fundamental questions about the nature of existence, the human mind, and the pursuit of self-knowledge.

He has written numerous thought-provoking books on self-discovery, the evolution of medicine, and human conditioning. His engagement with Advaita Vedanta and Indian philosophical traditions informs his approach, allowing him to distill complex metaphysical ideas into clear, practical insights. His works have been recognized for their ability to bridge ancient teachings with modern understanding, making them accessible to readers seeking both intellectual and experiential wisdom.

～

www.ingramcontent.com/pod-product-compliance
Lightning Source LLC
Chambersburg PA
CBHW051233130726
47988CB00001B/338